Medals of America

presents

Decorations, Medals, Ribbons, Badges and Insignia of the United States Air Force

The First 50 Years

By

Lt. Col. Anthony "Tony" A
USAF (Ret.)

1st Edition

Dedicated to America's finest veterans who served with integrity and dedication in the Army Air Corps, Army Air Force, and United States Air Force and to the families who supported them.
Aim High!

Library of Congress Catalog Card Number - 96-076064
Hardcover Edition ISBN - 1-884452-20-5
Softcover Edition ISBN - 1-884452-21-3

Copyright 1997 by MOA Press

Published by:

MOA Press (Medals of America Press)
1929 Fairview Road
Fountain Inn, SC 29644-9137
Telephone: (864) 862-6051

Printed in the United States of America
by Keys Printing Company
Greenville, South Carolina

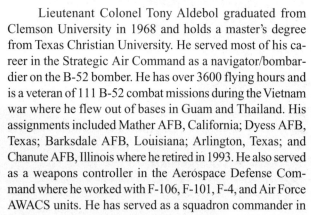

Utapao Air Base 1971

Lieutenant Colonel Tony Aldebol graduated from Clemson University in 1968 and holds a master's degree from Texas Christian University. He served most of his career in the Strategic Air Command as a navigator/bombardier on the B-52 bomber. He has over 3600 flying hours and is a veteran of 111 B-52 combat missions during the Vietnam war where he flew out of bases in Guam and Thailand. His assignments included Mather AFB, California; Dyess AFB, Texas; Barksdale AFB, Louisiana; Arlington, Texas; and Chanute AFB, Illinois where he retired in 1993. He also served as a weapons controller in the Aerospace Defense Command where he worked with F-106, F-101, F-4, and Air Force AWACS units. He has served as a squadron commander in Air Force Recruiting Service and as a group commander in Air Training/Air Education and Training Command. His decorations include the Distinguished Flying Cross, five Air Medals, and six Meritorious Service Medals. He is currently the customer service manager at Medals of America where he has become a leading authority on the decorations and awards for all services; he has often lectured at various veterans organizations providing insight and information on military awards. He and his wife, the former Avanette "Punkin" Walters currently reside in Greenville, South Carolina with their two children, Mandy and Jared.

Acknowledgements

I would like to express my appreciation to all those who provided me training, inspiration, and assistance in writing this book. First and foremost is Col. Frank Foster who convinced me that I could do this and without whose talents and direction this would have never been possible. I am indebted to Linda and Lee Foster, as well as Master Chief Jerry Dantzler, MT Dennis Phillips, and USMC First Sergeant Barbara Wamsley for their advice and encouragement.

I would like to thank the Air Force Historical Research Agency and the Air University Library at Maxwell Air Force Base, Alabama for providing access to the multitude of regulations from both the Army Air Force and U.S. Air Force periods, the major source of information for the book. The assistance of the U.S. Air Force Academy, most specifically Cadet Lisa Rockwell, is greatly appreciated in helping me to document their specific badge insignia. I'm deeply indebted to fellow authors Major Pete Morgan, Lonny Borts, and Jim Thompson for their insight and encouragement as well as for their assistance in obtaining some of the information for the book. A special thanks to Jan White for her technical assistance and cooperation without which this undertaking would not have occurred.

Thanks to the many veterans who have provided me insights and information through their phone calls, letters, and internet communications. Special thanks to Major Joseph Ward, comptroller squadron commander at Charleston AFB, for his invaluable inputs that gave me a clearer vision of the focus of this book.

I could not have completed this book without the unfaltering support of my wife, Punkin, who has endured many days and nights alone both during my 25 year Air Force career and during my close relationship with my computer. Thanks to all my family who continuously provided encouragement, especially my father, an Air Force veteran of 25 years and my father-in-law, an Air Force veteran of 27 years.

Last of all, my heartfelt thanks to the people with whom I served in the U.S. Air Force; their dedication, hard work, and loyalty to the mission as well as to their co-workers inspired me then as well as today.

Table of Contents

List of Illustrations

Introduction

After years of reading, studying, and collecting information on military rank, insignia, and badges, I realized that there is no one source for "complete" information on the rank insignia and badges of the U.S. Army Air Force and the U.S. Air Force. For the Air Force enthusiast, it is a difficult task to both locate and describe all the insignia of the AAF and the USAF. The term "Air Force" will be used throughout the book to indicate the AAF and the USAF, collectively, and the individual abbreviations, AAF and USAF, will be used to indicate specific service, when necessary.

As a member of the USAF for over 25 years, I still find it difficult to remember the rank structure of the enlisted corps, especially because of the many changes that have evolved. USAF rank insignia has recently undergone major changes that provoked a lot of opinions from both active duty and separated/retired Air Force personnel; indications are that Air Force rank insignia may stay the same for quite a while and could become "permanent." While I regret that we changed the rank structure that has basically been in place for over thirty years with the exception of changes in E-1 thru E-4 rank, I hope we will stick with a rank system that will strengthen our identity, pride, and heritage. I hope that this work will provide an accurate source for many years to come and will not become outdated as quickly as changes have been made to the Air Force rank structure over the last several years.

My main objective in this book is to document the insignia that has been worn by our valiant Air Force personnel from 1941 to the present. I may on occasion give my personal thought as to changes that have been made in badges and insignia.

There are many excellent references in the military book community that provide pictures, descriptions, and criteria for many of the insignia in this book; however, it is because of the lack of one comprehensive source on the subject of Air Force insignia that I have undertaken this project. I hope to provide the collector, the military historian, the veteran, and the occasional student of militaria, a single source for all Air Force insignia. I realize the pitfalls of using the word "complete" but I certainly worked under that premise to make this as "complete" a source as possible while knowing that just as soon as this book goes to print, I or someone else will discover something that I omitted. I welcome any additions, corrections, or other information that may possibly be included in a later edition. There are many variations of the different insignia presented here but my intent is to show just the basic insignia style and not to show the varied ways in which they were constructed; for an example, the basic pilot wing is shown but I know that there have been many different constructions of the same insignia.

I felt that a presentation of Army Air Force insignia was imperative since many of those personnel subsequently became U.S. Air Force personnel and also because there are so many World War II era veterans who are interested in obtaining and displaying the insignia that marked their distinguished uniforms of service. In my research I found many veterans who had forgotten or were just unsure about what their insignia was. Of course, some of today's Air Force badges, particularly some flight crew wings, remain the same basic design as they were during the AAF era.

A study of uniforms during both the AAF and USAF eras would be an appropriate complement to the material presented here but will not be attempted because of the magnitude of information available. The reader is encouraged to seek out regulations of the period and other historical sources to provide a complete picture of the Air Force uniform. I have likewise avoided a detailed discussion of patch insignia that would also easily comprise a work of its own; however, I will show and discuss some AAF and USAF patches and badges, such as the technical specialists badges, that are constructed of patch material and were worn on the enlisted AAF uniform. Prior to presenting the main focus of this book, Air Force decorations, awards, rank and badge insignia, I felt that it was appropriate to give some basic background information on both the AAF and the USAF to insure that the reader knows exactly what period is being referred to and the associated reference dates of the particular period, AAF vs USAF. My primary motivation for this book was to provide a source for those airmen who are interested in reconstructing the symbols of their dedicated service to the Air Force in order to provide themselves and their families an accurate and lasting commemoration of their service to the Air Force and the nation. AIM HIGH!

Tony Aldebol
Lt Col, USAF Retired
Greenville, South Carolina

Background

The actual beginning of badge, patch, and decoration insignia is impossible to pinpoint although most certainly rank insignia and uniforms were an important part of the success of the British Navy as far back as the 12th century. The historically successful French and Spanish armies from previous centuries also contributed to the establishment of insignia to enhance morale and promote efficiency.

Our system of recognizing significant accomplishments of our military personnel began with the Badge of

1782 Badge of Military Merit

Military Merit, designed by George Washington to recognize three patriots of the Revolutionary War. The Badge of Military Merit would later become the Purple Heart in 1932. The current decoration system has its roots in the initiative of the first President to recognize deserving service and would be firmly implanted during the Civil War when the first Medals of Honor would be presented.

The beginning of insignia for the "air arm" of the United States military began on August 1, 1907 when the Aeronautical Division of the U.S. Army Signal Corps was established to handle all military aviation matters and possible applications of air power. The first aviators wore the insignia of the Signal Corps on their collars and would eventually have unofficial wings added to the center of the Signal Corps badges. The first specifications for a military airplane were issued on December 23, 1907 by the Army's Chief Signal Officer, Brigadier General James Allen. On May 19, 1908, Lieutenant Thomas E. Selfridge became the first military person to fly an aircraft; a few months later, Lt. Selfridge also became the first military aviator to be killed in a powered aircraft accident at Fort Myers, Virginia. On January 19, 1910, Lt. Paul Beck became the first aviator to conduct a successful bombing mission when he dropped three sandbags on a target in Los Angeles, Ca.

The first military aviator badge was created on May 27, 1913 prior to the creation of the Aviation Section of the Signal Corps on July 18, 1914. The aviator badge was initially intended as an award and not a qualification badge. In 1916, the 1st Aero Squadron supported military operations led by General John J. Pershing against the infamous Pancho Villa in Mexico. On February 5, 1918 Lt. Stephen Thompson became

the first American aviator to shoot down an enemy aircraft; while flying as a gunner with a French pilot, he shot down a German Albatross. Lieutenant Paul Baer became the first American Expeditionary Force Air Service member to receive the Army Distinguished Service Cross on March 11, 1918.

After recognizing a need (and desire) to give our growing group of aviators an identifying badge, qualification badges were authorized in 1917. These initial badges would be the forerunner of today's pilot wings. The initial badge created was the Military Aviator badge with its two wings and the U.S. shield in the middle. A Junior Military Aviator badge was also created with the U.S. Shield and only one wing; the single wing design would eventually be discarded in favor of the double wing design that remains today.

On May 24, 1918, President Woodrow W. Wilson created the U.S. Army Air Service and placed it directly under the War Department. Four months later, Captain Eddie Rickenbacker became the first military aviator to earn the Medal of Honor for an air action over France. A gallery of famous aviators, such as General Billy Mitchell and Lt. James Doolittle, set flying records and strengthed the status of the fledgling Army Air Service. They too would be recognized by decorations for outstanding service and heroism. At the same time, air units were becoming cohesive and spirited organizations drawn together by an excitement of flying and an eagerness to serve.

Individual units began developing their own insignia usually painted on their aircraft and soon to become patches on their sleeves. By the time World War I was over, the Army Air Service had grown to more than 19,000 officers and 178,000 enlisted men before the rapid demobilization after the war.

Campaign and service medals had become firmly established as symbols of patriotic military service during the Spanish American War. At the time of the U. S. entry into World War I, the Medal of Honor, Certificate of Merit and Navy/Marine Good Conduct Medal represented America's entire inventory of personal decorations. This presented the twin dangers that the Medal of Honor might be cheapened by being awarded too often and that other deeds of valor might go unrecognized.

By 1918, popular interest brought two new awards, the Army's Distinguished Service Cross and Distinguished Service Medal, created by Executive Order in 1918. In the same year, the traditional U. S. refusal to permit the armed forces to accept foreign decorations was rescinded, allowing military personnel to accept awards from the grateful Allied governments.

Army DSC

The World War I Victory Medal provided a means to show recognition of our servicemen and the campaigns in which they fought. The issuance of the World War I Victory medal established another precedent, that of wearing clasps with the names of individual battles on the suspension ribbon of a campaign medal. This was an ongoing practice in many countries, most notably Britain and France, since the 19th Century. When the ribbon bar alone was worn, each clasp was represented by a small (3/16" diameter) bronze star. Fourteen such clasps were adopted along with five clasps to denote service in specific countries. During this same period, the Army used a 3/16" diameter silver star to indicate a citation for gallantry during any previous campaign, dating back to the Civil War. An officer or enlisted man so cited was also presented with a Silver Star citation, which evolved into the Silver Star Medal in 1932.

World War I Victory Medal with Ribbon Bars

On July 2, 1926 in the Air Corps Act of 1926, the Army Air Service became the U.S. Army Air Corps (USAAC) and a training center was established at Randolph Field near San Antonio, Texas. When Brigadier General Henry H. (Hap) Arnold was named Chief of the Army Air Corps on September 29, 1938, the Air Corps rank, badge, and patch insignia were firmly entrenched as symbols of authority, duties, and organization.

The Purple Heart would be revived in 1932 to recognize those who had been wounded in combat, replacing the wound stripes that had been worn to show wounds received during the first World War.

More military aviator badges were developed to recognize the different duties that

had evolved within aviation such as the navigator, observer, flight engineer, and bombardier in addition to the pilot. In 1939, President Roosevelt authorized over 3200 officers and 45,000 enlisted personnel for the AAC which remained one of the Army's combat arms.

The United States Army Air Forces (USAAF) was established on June 20, 1941 and became a co-equal to the Army Ground Forces. The USAAF was a part of the U.S. Army although it operated as an autonomous unit. Being a part of the U.S. Army, its airmen wore some of the same uniforms and insignia as their ground counterparts; primary differences were, of course, the flight uniforms, flight badges, and AAF patch insignia. Though technically incorrect, many AAF personnel then as well as today continue to refer to the

AAF as the Air Corps or Army Air Corps.

World War II saw a significant increase in both personal decorations and campaign medals. Since U. S. forces were serving all over the world, a campaign medal was designed for each major (and carefully defined) area. The three medals for the American, Asiatic-Pacific and European-African-Middle Eastern Campaigns represented military service around the globe. However, the World War I practice of using campaign bars was discarded in favor of 3/16" bronze stars that could denote any military endeavor, from a major invasion to a submarine war patrol.

During World War II, the first (and only!) service medal unique to female military personnel was introduced. Known as the Women's Army Corps Service Medal, it was authorized for service in both the W.A.C. and its predecessor, the Women's Army Auxiliary Corps. In addition, the war saw the large scale award of foreign medals and decorations to American servicemen. The Philippine Government, for one, authorized awards to commemorate the Defense and Liberation of their island country. The first foreign award designed strictly for units, the Philippine Presidential Unit Citation, patterned after a similar American award, was also approved for wear by American forces at this time. In the

European Theater, France and Belgium made many presentations of their War Crosses (Croix de Guerre) to U. S. military personnel.

On December 7, 1941 the Japanese bombed Pearl Harbor and nine days later Lt. Boyd Wagner became the first USAAF ace of World War II when he shot down his fifth Japanese plane over the Philippines. The AAF rapidly grew to a peak of over two million personnel after Pearl Harbor. Lt. Col. James (Jimmy) H. Doolittle led a squadron of B-25s on a raid over Tokyo on April 18, 1942. On July 4, 1942, the 97th Bombardment Group launched the first USAAF bombing mission in the European Theater. Ribbons were created for the uniform to show military participation prior to Pearl Harbor and service in the European and Pacific Theaters. Air Medals and Distinguished Flying Crosses were awarded in significant numbers to recognize flight accomplishments during the most treacherous of conditions.

On December 9, 1942, the AAF was designated an autonomous unit of the U.S. Army. Lt. Gen Hap Arnold became the AAF's first four star general on March 19, 1943. On December 21, 1944, Hap Arnold became the first airman to hold five-star rank when he was appointed General of the Army.

In October of 1942, a flight training program was started within the Army to

provide women pilots to help deliver aircraft from factories to airfields. In August of 1943, this organization of women pilots of the Army Air Forces became WASPs (Women's Airforce Service Pilots), previously called WAFS (Women's Auxiliary Ferrying Squadron). The WASP was deactivated in December 1944 after producing more than a thousand pilots to help the AAF during World War II. The WASP were granted veteran status by Congress in 1978. The WASP wore a blue wool gabardine uniform with an AAF shoulder patch along with the wings they were presented upon graduation from flight training. The WASP were always considered civilians in uniform until they achieved their well deserved recognition as veterans in 1978.

In July 1943, women were authorized to join the Women's Army Corps (WAC); in 1945, there were over 40,000 WAC personnel serving with the USAAF. In June 1948, women were permitted to join the U.S. Air Force when Congress passed the Women's Armed Services Integration Act and were known as WAF (Women in the Air Force). There were approximately 1500 women from the Army, Navy, and Marines who became the first members of the WAF. The WAF directorate was dissolved in June 1976. WAF wore the same rank insignia designs and badges as their male counterparts.

The United States Air Force (USAF) became a military service equal to the Army and Navy on September 18, 1947. The USAF began developing its own distinctive uniform but continued to hold on to the Army uniform and much of its insignia until the early 1950s. Except for a few of the Army badges, such as parachute badges, aircrew wings were the only badges authorized for the uniform during this period. Stuart Symington became the first Secretary of the Air Force and General Carl A. Spaatz became the United States Air Force's first Chief of Staff on September 26, 1947. The USAF's first major operation was the Berlin Airlift from June 26, 1948 to September 30, 1949 when it delivered over 2,000,000 tons of supplies to the isolated city.

On June 27, 1950, the USAF achieved it first air victories in the Korean War. The USAF uniform and insignia remained in a transitional state during the Korean War. There was a mix of Air Force and Army insignia and uniforms during the period. It was not uncommon to see USAF stripes on an Army uniform or Army insignia on an USAF uniform. The new "blue" Air Force uniform would not become firmly established until the end of the Korean War.

The National Defense Service Medal was instituted to recognize those who served during the Korean War. A Korean War Service Medal was authorized for those who served in Korea along with a United Nations Service Medal, the first time a UN medal was authorized to recognize service on behalf of the UN.

When the Korean War started in 1950, the fledgling new service, while trying to establish its new identity, still looked a lot like the U.S. Army. It was very difficult to see the difference between an "airman" and a "soldier" since many still wore the same Army uniform although the Air Force had adopted its blue uniform in January 1949. It was not until 1950 that most Air Force members would have the blue uniform that was agreed upon by Secretary of the Air Force Stuart Symington and Air Force Chief of Staff, General Carl Spatz in 1947. The first Air Force uniform was known as "shade 84 blue" and it had silver buttons on the coat, each containing the Air Force seal. The material used for the Air Force uniform has evolved over the last 50 years from the heavy woolen material used in the first uniforms to the present day comfortable polyester blend. While the basic designs of the pants and coat have remained essentially the same, the Air Force did experiment with other uniform combinations such as the khaki bush jacket with khaki shorts, black knee socks, and a pith helmet. The original tan khakis, called "505s" were replaced with a more easily maintained khaki called "1505s". There was a lot of jubilation when the khakis met their demise and were replaced with the long and short sleeve light blue shirts which were certainly easier to wash and iron. The Air Force blue shirt has undergone several modifications to incorporate both metal and epaulet rank insignia and the wear of a tie in some combinations. The smooth professional appearance of the uniform today is in stark contrast to the "difficult to maintain" khaki uniforms of the past. A major break from Air Force uniform tradition was averted when Chief of Staff, General Ronald Fogleman, abandoned the short-lived "airline" uniform of the early 1990s in favor of the more traditional style with rank insignia of the same style as had been used by the AAF and USAF previously. Many personnel did not even wear the airline style uniform before it was "canned." The current style uniform reflects the tradition of the first USAF uniform and to me is the uniform that is "Air Force" and should be kept with possibly only minor future modifications. While there have been some changes in the blue of the uniform, I won't be too unhappy as long as we keep it "Blue!"

On April 1, 1954, President Dwight D. Eisenhower signed into law a bill creating the United States Air Force Academy; the Academy swore in its first class on July 11, 1955. The Academy, Officer Training School, and Air Force ROTC have used the current style blue uniform with their individual cadet rank insignia attached. With the creation of the Air Force Commendation Medal in 1958, the Air Force saw the beginning of medals created uniquely for Air Force personnel. The early 60s saw the addition of the Air Force Cross, the Air Force Distinguished Service Medal, the Airman's Medal, the Combat Readiness Medal, the Air Force Good Conduct Medal, and the Air Reserve Forces Meritorious Service Medal to the list of USAF awards.

The Vietnam War period saw the transition begin from  the khaki style uniforms to the dark blue pants/skirts with light blue shirts and blouses. The early 1980s saw the appearance of epaulet rank for the uniform short and long sleeve shirts, replacing the pin-on rank of the previous shirts and blouses. Additional Air Force awards were created in the 80s, including the Air Force Achievement Medal and several ribbon awards for service, training,

and recognition.

The uniform insignia stabilized until after Operation Desert Storm (The Gulf War) and the end of the cold war. The Air Force underwent a major reorganization after the cold war, consolidating from thirteen to eight major commands.

In 1996, total active duty Air Force strength was less than 400,000 personnel. The USAF continues to support NATO operations in the Balkans after participating in peacekeeping and humanitarian operations in Somalia, Rwanda, and Haiti. Recent service medals have been created for those who served in these areas, including the NATO Medal, the Armed Forces Service Medal, and individual United Nations Medals for specific operations.

Many of the badges and insignia of the Army Air Corps and Army Air Force were removed from the new Air Force uniform in an effort to make the uniform as uncluttered as possible. The officer and enlisted uniform were the same except for the rank insignia and the minor difference of "U.S." within a circle on the lapels of the enlisted uniform and the "uncircled 'U.S.'" on the officer uniform lapels. The wing design of General Hap Arnold was retained for the pilot wing badge.

The USAF has had difficulty resolving the enlisted rank structure since its inception; the primary problem being the exact line where the Airmen ranks should stop and where the noncommissioned officer (NCO) ranks should begin. The stripe situation to this date remains a point of confusion to those long since separated/retired as well as to many that are still on active duty.

The officer rank has remained basically the same; changes have revolved around how they were displayed (epaulet with rank embroidered versus metal rank). The obvious exception to this is the rank of the warrant officer grades which have changed radically in design from those worn in the AAF to those worn in the USAF until the demise of the warrant grades within the Air Force. Numerous specialty badges have been added during the last several years. It is inevitable that more will be added and perhaps some deleted as roles and missions change.

The 50th anniversary of the United States Air Force is an excellent time to reflect on where we started, where we are, and where we are going. Our history is not only told by our accomplishments but also on the uniforms and insignia. Air Force insignia is an important part of our history and will continue to tell the Air Force story into the next 50 years and beyond. Badges and insignia will change but the men and women behind that insignia will continue to keep us a leader in world air power.

Issue of U.S. Medals to Veterans, Retirees, and Their Families

The Air Force normally issues decorations and service medals as they are awarded or earned. The Air Force does not issue or replace any foreign awards, only United States awards.

Veterans of any U. S. military service may request replacement of medals which have been lost, stolen, destroyed or rendered unfit through no fault of the recipient. Requests may also be filed for awards that were earned but, for any reason, were never issued to the service member. The next-of-kin of deceased veterans may also make the same request.

AIR FORCE — The Air Force processes requests for medals through the National Personnel Records Center, which determines eligibility through the information in the veteran's records. Once verified, a notification of entitlement is forwarded to Randolph Air Force Base, Texas, from which the medals are mailed to the requestor. To request medals earned while in the Air Force or its predecessor, the Army Air Corps, veterans or their next-of-kin should write to:

National Personnel Records Center
Air Force Reference Branch
9700 Page Avenue
St. Louis, MO 63132-5100

Where to write in case of a problem or an appeal and where medals are mailed from:

Headquarters
Air Force Personnel Center
AFPC/DPPPR
550 C Street West, Suite 12
Randolph AFB, TX 78150-4714

It is recommended that requesters use Standard Form 180, *Request Pertaining to Military Records*, when applying. Forms are available from offices of the Department of Veterans Affairs (VA). If the Standard Form 180 is not used, a letter may be sent, but it must include: the veteran's full name used while in service, the branch of service, approximate dates of service, and service number. The letter should indicate if the request is for a specific medal(s), or for all medals earned. The letter must be signed by the veteran or his next-of-kin, indicating the relationship to the deceased.

It is also helpful to include copies of any military service documents that indicate eligibility for medals, such as military orders or the veteran's report of separation (DD Form 214 or its earlier equivalent).

The DD Form 214, Report of Separations, is filed in the Official Military Personnel Record File. Copies of the DD214 can be made available upon request.

Veterans and next-of-kin of deceased veterans have the same rights to full access to the record. Next-of-kin are the unremarried widow or widower, son or daughter, father or mother, brother or sister of the deceased veteran.

Authorized third party requesters, e.g., lawyers, doctors, historians, etc., may submit requests for information from individual records with the veteran's (or next-of-kin's) signed and dated authorization. All authorizations should specify exactly what the veteran (or next-of-kin) is allowing to be released to a third party. Authorizations are valid one year from date of signature.

Information or copies of documents may be released from Official Military Personnel Files within the provisions of the law. The Freedom of Information Act (FOIA) and the Privacy Act provide balance between the right of the public to obtain information from military service records, and the right of the former military service member to protect his/her privacy. Please review these items for additional information. In all cases, you must sufficiently identify the person whose record is requested, so that the records can be located with reasonable effort.

Federal law [5 USC 552a(b)] requires that all requests for information from official military personnel files be submitted in writing. Each request must be signed (in cursive) and dated (within the last year). For this reason, no requests are accepted over the internet.

Requests must contain enough information to identify the record among the more than 70 million on file at NPRC (MPR). Certain basic information is needed to locate military service records. This information includes the veteran's complete name used while in service, service number or social security number, branch of service, and dates of service. Date and place of birth may also be helpful, especially if the service number is not known. If the request pertains to a record that may have been involved in the 1973 fire at NPRC (MPR), also include place of discharge, last unit of assignment, and place of entry into the service, if known.

The Center may have a difficult time locating your records since millions of records were lost in a fire at the National Personnel Records Center in 1973. The fire destroyed 80 per cent of the Army's discharge records between November 1912 and December 1959. World War II Army Air Force records were in this group. Seventy-five per cent of Air Force discharge records before 1964 and whose last names that fall alphabetically between Hubbard (James E.) and Z were also burned. Only four million records from this period were saved. Although the requested medals can often be issued on the basis of alternate records, the documents sent in with the request are sometimes the only means of determining proper eligibility.

Finally, requesters should exercise extreme patience. It may take several months or, in some cases, a year to determine eligibility and dispatch the appropriate medals. The Center asks that you not send a follow-up request for 90 days. Due to these delays, many veterans simply purchase their medals from a supplier.

Wear of Medals, Insignia and the Uniform by Veterans, Retirees and Former Service Members

INTRODUCTION

One of the first lessons taught to new recruits is proper wear of the uniform and its insignia. The same principal applies to wear of military awards on their old uniform by veterans and retirees. There are a number of occasions when tradition, patriotism, ceremonies and social occasions call for the wear of military awards.

CIVILIAN DRESS

The most common manner of wearing a decoration or medal is as a lapel pin in the left lapel buttonhole of a civil-

ian suit jacket. The small enameled lapel pin represents the ribbon bar of a single decoration or ribbon an individual has received (usually the highest award or one having special meaning to the wearer). Many well known veterans such as former Senator Bob Dole, a World War II Purple Heart recipient, wear a lapel pin. Pins are available for all awards and some ribbons such as the Marine Combat Action Ribbon or Presidential Unit Citation.

Small miniature wings are also worn in the lapel or as a tie tac. Additionally, retirees are encouraged to wear their USAF retired pin and World War II veterans are encouraged to wear their Honorable Discharge Pin (affectionally referred to as the "ruptured duck").

WW II Honorable Discharge Button

Air Force Retired Pin

Honorably discharged and retired Air Force members may wear full-size or miniature medals on civilian suits on appropriate occasions such as Memorial Day and Armed Forces Day. Female members may wear full-size or miniature medals on equivalent dress. It is not considered appropriate to wear skill or qualification badges on civilian attire.

FORMAL CIVILIAN WEAR

For more formal occasions, it is correct and encouraged to wear miniature decorations and medals. For a black or white tie occasion, the rule is quite simple: if the lapel is wide enough wear the miniatures on the left lapel or, in the case of a shawl lapel on a tuxedo, the miniature medals are worn over the left breast pocket. The center of the holding bar of the bottom row of medals should be parallel to the ground immediately above the pocket. Do not wear a pocket handkerchief. Miniature medals make a handsome statement of patriotic service at weddings and other social events.

Miniature medals can also be worn on a civilian suit at veterans' functions, memorial events, formal occasions of ceremony and social functions of a military nature.

WEAR OF THE UNIFORM

On certain occasions retired Air Force personnel may wear either the uniform prescribed at the date of retirement or any of the current active duty authorized uniforms. Retirees should adhere to the same grooming standards as Air Force active duty personnel when wearing the Air Force uniform (for example, a beard is inappropriate while in uniform). When ever the uniform is worn, it must be done in such a manner as to reflect credit upon the individual and the service from which he/she is retired. (Do not mix uniform items.)

The occasions are for wear by retirees are :
- military ceremonies
- military funerals, weddings, memorial services and inaugurals
- patriotic parades on national holidays
- military parades in which active or reserve units are participating
- educational institutions when engaged in giving military instruction or responsible for military discipline
- social or other functions when the invitation has obviously been influenced by the members at one time being in active military service

Honorably separated wartime veterans may wear the uniform authorized at the time of their service.

The occasions are:
- military funerals, memorial services, and inaugurals
- patriotic parades on national holidays
- military parades in which active or reserve units are taking part
- any occasion authorized by law

Non war-time service personnel separated (other than retired, ANG and Reserve) are not authorized to wear the uniform but may wear the medals.

Service Dress Uniform prior to 1996

(Mandatory) Place "US" letters halfway up the seam, resting on but not over it. Bottom of the US insignia is horizontal with the ground. (Enlisted "US" is shown on left collar)

Foreign badges (aviation, medical insignia, parachutist badges) center 1/2 inch above name tag. Wear in same relative position when not wearing name tag. (Must wear corresponding U.S. badge)

(Optional) Center name tag over but not on top of edge of pocket, between left and right edges.

(Optional) Center badge on the lower portion of pocket between left and right edges and bottom of flap and pocket.

Aeronautical and chaplain badges are mandatory. Others are optional. Center occupational badge 1/2 inch above the top row of ribbons. Center aeronautical badge 1/2 inch above occupational badge.

(Mandatory) Center ribbons over but not on top of edges of welt pocket. Wear three or four in a row.

(Mandatory) Center sleeve chevron halfway between shoulder seam and elbow bent at 90-degree angle. Wear new style rank insignia on new service dress coat only.

Center duty or miscellaneous badge 1 1/2 inches below top of welt pocket.

Wear of Decorations, Medals and Insignia by Active Duty, National Guard and Reserve Personnel

General Guide

prior to 1996

Service Ribbons — Ribbons are worn on service dress and blue shirt. Ribbons are normally worn in rows of three with the bottom bar centered and resting on the top edge of the pocket. Ribbons may be worn four-in-a-row with the left edge of the ribbons aligned with the left edge of pocket to keep lapel from covering ribbons. There is no space between rows of ribbons.

Full Size Medals — Normally worn three to a row, but may be overlapped up to five medals on a 2 3/4 inch holding bar. No medal should be overlapped more than 50% and the medal nearest the lapel should be fully exposed. Six medals should be displayed in two rows, three over three. Regular size medals are worn on the service dress and ceremonial dress uniforms with the medal portion of the bottom row immediately above the top of the pocket button.

Miniature Medals — Miniature Medals are worn on the blue mess dress or on formal dress. The miniatures are centered between lapel and arm seam and midway between top shoulder seam and top button of jacket. If more than four miniatures, the wearer has the option of mounting up to seven by overlapping or going to a 2nd bar. Seven is the maximum on one bar, however, many in the Air Force prefer only a maximum of four to a bar.

Long and Short Sleeve Shirts

(Mandatory) Officers place shoulder mark insignia as close as possible to shoulder seam. Airmen center current 3-inch or new 3 1/2 inch sleeve chevron halfway between shoulder seam and bottom edge of sleeve (short-sleeved) or elbow when bent at 90-degree angle. Senior noncommissioned officers (SNCO) wear shoulder mark insignia or chevrons. Wear the current or new style rank insignia.

Foreign badges (aviation, medical insignia, parachutist badges) center 1/2 inch above name tag. Wear in same relative position when not wearing name tag.*

(Mandatory) Center name tag over but not on top of edge of pocket.

Center badge on the lower portion of pocket and between left and right edges and bottoms of flap and pocket.

*Wear only in conferring country at official or social functions. Must wear corresponding U.S. badge.

Aeronautical and chaplain badges are mandatory. Others are optional. Center badge 1/2 inch above top row of ribbons or pocket if not wearing ribbons. Center additional badge 1/2 inch above first badge.

(Optional) Center ribbons over but not on top of edge of pocket and between the left and right edges.

(Optional) Center badge on the lower portion of pocket between left and right edges and bottoms of flap and pocket.

(Optional) Center tie tack or tie clasp between bottom edge of knot and bottom tip of tie. Always wear tie with long sleeve shirt.

Service Dress Uniform

(Mandatory) Place "US" letters halfway up the seam, resting on but not over it. Bottom of the US insignia is horizontal with the ground.

Epaulets with officer shoulder sleeve insignia replaced aluminum sleeve rank, effective 1 Oct 1996. (Mandatory) Center new sleeve chevron halfway between shoulder seam and elbow bent at 90-degree angle. Wear new style rank insignia on new service dress coat. —

(Optional) Center badge on the lower portion of pocket 1 1/2 inches below top of pocket welt. If a duty/misc badge is worn on the right side, it should be worn with bottom edge of the badge parallel to the top of the welt pocket.

Aeronautical and chaplain badges are mandatory. Others are optional. Center occupational badge 1/2 inch above the top row of ribbons. Center aeronautical badge 1/2 inch above occupational badge. Center duty or miscellaneous badge 1 1/2 inches below top of welt pocket. Wear highly polished badges only.

(Mandatory) Center ribbons over but not on top of edges of welt pocket. Wear three or four in a row. Individuals may wear all or some of their authorized ribbons. (Name tags are not authorized on this uniform)

Dress and Formal Dress

1. Aeronautical and chaplain badges are mandatory. Others are optional. Center 1/2 inch above top row of medals, or when not authorized medals, midway between shoulder and top button. Wear either highly polished or satin finished badges, cuff links or studs. Wear cuff links and studs as a set. Do not mix chrome or satin finish.

2. (Mandatory) Center miniature medals between lapel and arm seam and midway between top shoulder seam and top button of jacket.

3. (Optional) Center duty/misc badge (missile badge shown) 1/2 inch below bottom row of medals or comparable position when no medals are authorized.

4. (Mandatory) Officers: Place shoulder board insignia as close as possible to shoulder seam. Airmen: Center 4-inch chevron (either aluminum color on blue background or new style rank insignia) halfway between shoulder seam and elbow bent at 90-degree angle.

Special note: Blue satin bow tie worn with mess dress, white bow tie with formal dress.

Displaying Military Awards

In the United States, it is quite rare for an individual to wear full-size medals once no longer on active duty. Unfortunately, many veterans return to civilian life with little concern for the state of their awards. In the excitement of the transition, medals and badges are tucked away in drawers or children play with them, often causing irreparable damage to these noble symbols of a man's or woman's patriotic deeds. The loss or damage of these medals is sad, since the medals and badges reflect the veteran's part in American history and are totally unique and personal to each family.

The most appropriate use of military medals after active service is to mount the medals for permanent display in home or office. This reflects the individual's patriotism and the service rendered the United States. Unfortunately, there are very few first class companies in the United States who possess the expertise to properly prepare and mount awards and other personal militaria. The following pages provide examples of the formats, mounting methods and configurations employed by Medals of America, Limited in Fountain Inn, South Carolina to display military decorations. The examples range from World War II to the present.

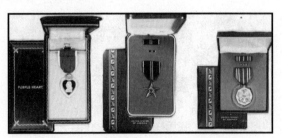

Decorations are usually awarded in a presentation set which normally consists of a medal, ribbon bar and lapel pin, all contained in a special case. During World War II, the name of the decoration was stamped in gold on the front of the case. However, as budget considerations assumed greater importance, this practice was gradually phased out and replaced by a standard case with "United States of America" emblazoned on the front.

At the present time, the more common decorations, (e.g., Achievement and Commendation Medals), come in small plastic cases, suitable only for initial presentation and storage of the medal. Using this case in its open position for prolonged display exposes the entire presentation set to dust, acids and other atmospheric contaminants which can cause tarnish and/or serious discoloration.

Outside the case, medals and ribbons should be handled as little as possible, since oils and dirt on the hands can cause oxidation on the pendant and staining of the ribbon.

The most effective method of protecting awards involves the use of a shadow box or glass display case with at least 1/2 inch between the medals and the glass. This provides a three dimensional view and protects the medal display in a dust-free environment. Cases which press the medals and ribbons against the glass can disfigure the ribbon, cause discoloration and, in some extreme cases, damage the medal.

The greatest mistake an ordinary frame shop can make is in the actual process of mounting the medals. They often clip off prongs or pins on the back of a medal to ease the task of gluing the medal to a flat surface. The physical alteration destroys the integrity of the medal and the use of glues ruins the back of the ribbon and medal. The net result, ignoring the intrinsic value of the piece, is serious damage to a valued heirloom and keepsake.

The best way to mount medals is in a wooden case especially designed for that purpose. They can be obtained either with a fold-out easel back for placement on a table, desk or mantle, or with a notched hook on the rear of the wooden frame for hanging on a wall. The case should also have brass turnbuckles on the back to facilitate removal of the mounting board for close examination of the medals or rearrangement of the displayed items.

The mounting board is absolutely critical. Velvet, flan-

The blue background case shows aerial gunner wings over aircrew wings of an 8th Air Force Veteran. The medals are: Air medal, Army Good Conduct, American Campaign, European Theater (ETO), and Victory Medal. Brass S/Sgt insignia and Air Corps branch insignia flank the name plate with an Honorable Discharge pin and Presidential Unit Citation above.

nel and old uniforms, just don't do the job. A first class mounting system starts with acid-free Befang or Gator board at least 1/4 inch thick. This board is very sturdy, being composed of two layers of hard, white paper board sandwiched around a foam core. Over this, a high quality velour-type material to which velcro will adhere is glued and pressed down evenly. The medals are mounted using velcro tape; one piece over the ribbon mounting pin and one, about the size of a nickel, on the medal back. The velcro locks the medal very firmly into place without causing any damage and alleviates the need to cut off the pin backs. Badges or ribbon bars with pin backs can be mounted by pressing the prongs through the fabric into the gator board, which moulds around the prongs. A little velcro tape on the back of the pronged device adds extra holding power.

Patches, brass plates, dog tags and other mementos can easily be added this way. The great beauty of this method is found not only in its eye appeal, but also that one can add to the display or rearrange the existing contents by gently peeling the medal off as simply as opening a velcro zipper. Prong devices can also be moved easily, since the foam core closes in behind the prong as it is removed, thus effectively sealing the hole once more.

The final element in the process is the frame itself. While oak and other heavy woods make very handsome pieces of furniture, they are not a good choice for a frame. The frame's weight puts a great strain on modern plasterboard walls when an extensive medal display is attached via standard hooks and nails. In addition, handling a heavy frame by very young or very old hands increases the chance it could

be accidentally dropped. For these reasons, frames should be milled from a lightweight wood with good staining characteristics. Bass wood is considered the best for the purpose and some poplar is acceptable. Metal frames, on the other hand, should be avoided, owing to their heavy weight and to the bright coloring which can conflict with the patina of the medals. Finally, the wood stain, (e.g., walnut stain), should reflect a rich, warm glow to properly envelop and enhance the medal display.

An essential part of the display case is the brass plate which provides the key information pertaining to the recipient of the displayed awards. This is definitely a place where one should not cut corners. A bargain basement brass or gold colored plastic nameplate will cheapen and distract from an otherwise elegant display case. Conversely, a high quality brass plate with good quality engraving will forever enhance the dignity of the medal display.

Whenever possible, the engraved letters should be blackened to provide enhanced contrast and visibility. The plate should, as a minimum, contain the full name, assigned unit and time frame. Other useful items are rank, service number and branch of the service if space permits. The contents of a nameplate are obviously a personal preference, but experience has shown that a limit of four or five lines can enhance and compliment the display, while a greater number of lines is a distraction.

Below and on the next page, are some examples of different display cases. Many of these examples are shown in color in the color plates.

This display of a 20th Air Force Pilot shows service in the Pacific. The Army Air Corps Hat insignia is positioned over the pilot wings. The medals are: Distinguished Flying Cross, Bronze Star, Purple Heart, Air Medal, (2nd row), American Campaign, Asiatic/Pacific, Victory and Philippine Liberation. A rank badge and metal branch insignia flank the name plate with an Honorable Discharge pin above.

USAF WWII & KOREA

This USAF Master Sergeant's display honors his service during WWII and Korea. The USAF bullion patch is surrounded by enamel pins of the units with which he served. Medals shown are: Army and AF Commendation, Army and AF Good Conduct, American Defense Service, American Campaign, European Theater, Victory, and the National Defense Service Medal. AF Longevity Service Award and Presidential Unit Citation are mounted above name plate flanked by metal old style Master Sergeant chevrons.

USAF Korean Service

This is a really handsome Korean War display case. A USAF Bullion patch is flanked by USAF collar insignia. The Army Good Conduct, National Defense, Korean Service and UN Korean Service and Korean Service Commemorative Medal. Korean Presidential Unit Citation is mounted above the name plate, flanked by metal rank. The Korean Commemorative medal is patterned after the Korean war service medal offered the U.S. by the Korean Government and turned down by the U.S.

USAF Vietnam Service

An officer's hat badge and wings top the medals: Distinguished Flying Cross, Meritorious Service, Air Medal, AF Commendation Medal, Combat Readiness, National Defense, Vietnam Service, RVN Staff Medal, and RVN Campaign. RVN Gallantry Cross Unit Citation is above the brass name plate flanked by officer rank insignia.

USAF Peacetime Service

This Airman's case uses a USAF bullion crest, a full set of ribbons and his skill badge. Medals are: AF Achievement, Good Conduct, and National Defense Service. Metal rank adds nice touch on either side of the brass name plate. Four ribbons that do not have medals are on the 7-ribbon bar: Overseas Short Tour, Air Force Longevity Service Award, Small Arms Expert Marksmanship, and Air Force Training Ribbon.

Early USAF Southwest Asia

This pilot's case uses a USAF enamel Crest flanked by his Captain's bars. His pilot wings are positioned over his medals as they would be if worn on the uniform. Medals are: the Distinguished Flying Cross, the Bronze Star for meritorious service, and the Air Medal. The second row has the National Defense Service, Southwest Asia Service, and the Saudi's Kuwait Liberation Medal. "US" lapel insignia adds nice touch on either side of the brass name plate. This is called an early Operation Desert Storm (ODS) case since the Kuwait Liberation of Kuwait Medal was not approved until sometime after the conflict. The case below displays the Kuwait Liberation of Kuwait Medal.

USAF Southwest Asia

This Senior NCO's case uses a USAF enamel medallion flanked by his metal rank insignia. Centered below is a full set of ribbons under his Security Police Badge. Medals are AF Commendation, AF Achievement, Good Conduct, National Defense, Southwest Asia Service, Saudi Kuwait Liberation and Kuwait Liberation of Kuwait Medal. The brass plates provides details that the awards and insignia do not tell.

Army Air Force (Army Air Corps) Insignia

Air Corps Cadet Cap Device

Cap insignia was an enlarged version of the officer's aviation branch insignia.

Aviation Cadet Reserve Lapel Button

The Aviation Cadet Reserve Service Lapel Pin was issued to every cadet in the Aviation Reserve program.

Pre Sept.8 ,1939 Pin

Officer Cap Device

Officers wore the large gold US Coat of Arms on the service cap.

World War II Honorable Discharge Pins

The Honorable Service Lapel Pin was issued to every service member that was honorably discharged between September 8, 1939 and December 31, 1946. More commonly known as the "ruptured duck" pin, it is a small brass emblem, 7/16 inch high and 5/8 inch wide. An initial design of the pin was for it to be made of blue plastic but a later regulation required it to be molded in gold-plated plastic which was later changed to gold-plated brass once metal restrictions were lifted after the war. A slightly different design was used for discharged personnel prior to Sept. 8, 1939.

Enlisted Cap Device

Enlisted personnel wore a brass disc on their wheel cap; the design on the disc was a US Coat of Arms. Some AAF personnel wore either branch insignia or distinctive unit insignia on the left front of their garrison cap.

U.S. Insignia

AAF officer "US" insignia was gold-colored and 7/16th inch high; it is the same size as current USAF "US" insignia. AAF enlisted "US" insignia contained the gold-colored letters "US" on a gold-colored disc. The "US" insignia was worn on the right collar by enlisted personnel and on both collars by officers. Cadets wore officer style branch insignia and U.S. devices on coat collars and lapels. Enlisted insignia were smaller versions of officers insignia and attached to a one inch diameter disk.

Warrant Officer Cap Device

The warrant officer hat insignia consists of an eagle rising with wings displayed, standing on two arrows and enclosed in a wreath. It was approved on May 12, 1921 and was first worn by warrant officers in the U.S. Army Tank Corps. The insignia was adopted from the great seal of the United States with the arrows symbolizing the military arts and sciences.

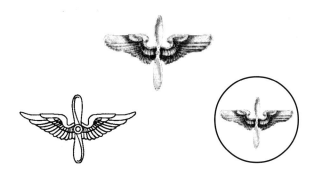

Aviation Branch Insignia

AAF aviation branch insignia is very similar to the aviation branch insignia used by the U.S. Army today. The difference in the two is the design of the wings. The insignia was patterned after the pilot badge of 1919 and the Aviation Cadet insignia authorized in 1933.

Officers wore the gold colored wing emblem (1 1/4 in wide) with a silver vertical propeller (3/4 in.) centered through the middle of the wing on each lapel centered below the "U.S." insignia which was worn on each collar of the service coat.

Enlisted personnel wore the circular brass disc with gold colored wings and propeller attached on the left collar of the AAF enlisted uniform. Like the US insignia of the period, they were originally made in a two-piece style, but in 1942 they began to make them in one piece out of brass-plated zinc.

Army Air Force Technician Specialists

Army Air Force Regulation 35-12 on March 1, 1943 created five categories of enlisted technical specialists and authorized the wearing of an ultramarine blue triangular patch to designate one of the five assigned occupational fields. The 2 1/2 in. equilateral triangle patch with the gold colored specialty emblem was worn centered on the outside of the right sleeve four inches above the lower edge of the sleeve of the coat, field jacket, and shirt; it was also worn on the left breast pocket of the fatigue uniform.

The five specified occupational fields were:

1. **Armament Specialist** which was denoted by a falling bomb. It was worn by nine occupations which included Aerial Torpedo Mechanic, Anti-aircraft Machine Gunner, and Bombsight Mechanic.

2. **Communications Specialist** which depicts a tower between four flashes. It was worn by 22 different occupational fields that included Radio Operator, Control Tower Operator, Communication Chief, Cryptographer, Radio Mechanics, Radio Observers, Telephone & Telegraph Lineman, and Wire Chief.

3. **Engineering Specialist** which shows the silhouette of an engine. It was worn by 33 different occupational fields including Airplane Inspector, Crew Chief, Line Chief, Flight Chief, Mechanical Specialist, Depot Engineer Chief, Parachute Shop Chief, Parachute Rigger and Repairman, Glider Mechanic, and Welder.

4. **Photography Specialist** which depicts a camera. It was worn by nine occupational specialties including Camera Technician, Photographic Chief, Photographic Interpeter, Photographic Laboratory Chief, and Motion Picture Cameraman.

5. **Weather Specialist** which depicts a weather vane. It was worn by six occupations including Weather Cryptographer, Forecaster, Observer, Station Chief, and Radio Sonde Operator.

AAF Patches

Unit patches were worn on the sleeve of the left shoulder (enlisted personnel wore them above the rank chevron). Examples of Army Air Force patch insignia are shown on the color plates and on pp. 52-53.

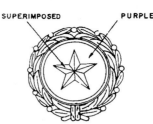

Distinctive Insignia

Unit distinctive insignia was worn by officers on the epaulet of the service coat and by enlisted men on the lower portion of the lapel.

Gold Star Lapel Pin

The Gold Star Lapel Button was established on August 1, 1947 to provide an appropriate identification for widows, widowers, parents, and next of kin of members of the Armed Forces who lost their lives while engaged in an action against an enemy of the United States. The pin consists of a gold star on a purple circular background, bordered in gold and surrounded by gold laurel leaves. On the reverse is the inscription, "United States of America, Act of Congress" with date "August 1947" or date "August 1966" and a space for engraving the initials of the recipient.

Service Stripes (Hash Marks)

Each stripe represents three years of honorable enlisted Federal service and is worn on the left sleeve at a 45 degree angle four inches from the end of the sleeve. Stripes were olive-drab, 2 1/4 inches long and 5/16 in. in width with a 1/8 in. border around the stripe.

Distinguished Aerial Gunnery Badge

Awarded to annual competition winners prior to World War II. The badge was gold and had a wreathed winged bullet suspended from a bar that bore the word "Distinguished."

Overseas Service Bars and World War I Wound and Service Chevrons

One service bar was authorized for each 6 months of active Federal service (for both enlisted and officer personnel) outside the continental limits of the United States in a combat theater. They are worn centered parallel on the left sleeve with the lowest bar four inches above the end of the sleeve. When worn with service stripes, they are worn above the uppermost service chevron.

Wound chevrons could be worn during World War II by those Army personnel authorized to do so for wounds received during World War I.

Service chevrons awarded for six months service in a theater of operations during World War I could also be worn during World War II.

Distinguished Aerial Bomber Badge

Awarded to annual competition winners prior to World War II. The badge was gold and had a wreathed bullseye with dropped bomb in its center and suspended from the bar that bore the word "Distinguished."

Glider Wings

Authorized March 14, 1944 for personnel trained in glider operations. Any service member who made one or more glider-borne combat landing into enemy held territory was authorized to wear it. Bronze stars are added to indicate more than one glider assault.

Technician Qualification Badge and Bars

Twenty four qualification bars were listed in AR 600-35, dated July 4, 1945 (27 shown). Bars were awarded for qualification in one of the designated specialities. The badge is silver and individuals with multiple qualifications wear the bars for each speciality suspended from the badge.

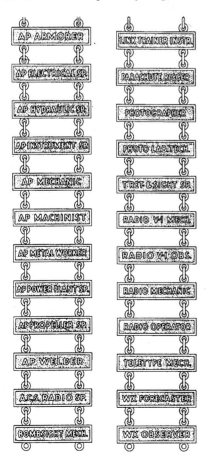

Badges for Gunnery and Marksmanship Qualification

Expert Basic Qualification Badge

Sharpshooter, 1st Class Gunner Badge

Marksman, 2nd Class Gunner Badge

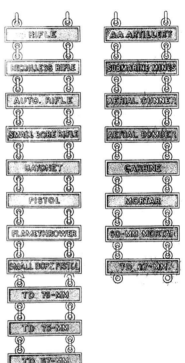

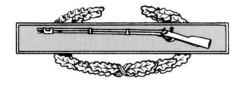

Combat Infantryman Badge (CIB)

The CIB was established by the War Department on Ocober 27, 1943, retroactive to December 7, 1941. It remains one of the most revered and coveted badges in the U.S. military. Details for the award of the CIB are covered on page 131.

Army Air Force Wings

The Military Aviator Badge was instituted on May 27, 1913 as an award, not as a qualification badge. It was made of 14 kt gold and depicted the American bald eagle in a diving position clutching the crossed flags of the Signal Corps in its talons; the eagle is suspended from a tablet that bears the words "Military Aviator." An initial requirement for the badge was for the individual to pilot an aircraft at least 2,500 feet above the ground.

In 1921, Army Regulation 600-35 authorized four aviation badges:

(1) Airplane Pilot

(2) Airship Pilot

(3) Airplane Observer

(4) Balloon Observer

An additonal badge, "Military Airplane Pilot," was added in 1937; this badge was usually called "Senior Pilot."

On February 20, 1940, the Airship Pilot Badge was abolished and the other badges were redesignated as Combat Observer, Pilot, and Balloon Pilot in addition to the Senior Pilot Badge. On March 23, 1940, four additional ratings were approved:
  (1) Command Pilot
  (2) Technical Observer
  (3) Senior Balloon Pilot
  (4) Balloon Observer.

During World War II, on September 4, 1942, the Combat Observer Wing was redesignated as "Aircraft Observer" and six additional wings were announced:
  (1) Navigator
  (2) Bombardier
  (3) Aircrew Member
  (4) Service Pilot
  (5) Liaison Pilot
  (6) Glider Pilot.

On April 29, 1943, the Aerial Gunner Badge was announced and in 1944, the Senior Service Pilot, Senior Aircraft Observer, and Flight Engineer badges were approved.

Commanders were the deciding authority during World War II whether or not World War I badges could be worn on the AAF uniform. Although many aircrew members during World War II were authorized more than one rating, they could only wear one set of wings. AAF and USAF wings have always been worn on the left breast of the uniform while wings awarded by foreign nations were worn on the right breast. Aircrew members have always had to meet established criteria to wear the wings for a particular aircrew position. Wings that were worn or authorized for wear by AAF flying personnel are listed below. USAF applicable wings are listed with USAF insignia.

Pilot Wings

The standard design of pilot wings that remains in use today was introduced on January 25, 1919 as the "Airplane Pilot Badge." The centerpiece of the wing is the Federal Shield which has been a symbol of the United States since early in its history. To be awarded this badge initially required not less than 200 hours of flying time and not less than 75 hours of that as solo time. It was redesignated as a "Pilot" Badge on February 20, 1940. The badge was made of oxidized silver and measured 3 1/8 inch across. Two inch wings were authorized for wear on shirts but were hardly ever worn during the AAF years; however, they have been used extensively in the USAF, especially from the 1960s forward. Sterling wings were common during World War II but gradually disappeared after the war. To be awarded the wings in the AAF, the individual must have completed AAF pilot training or have been recommended by a board of officers because of previous qualifications.

Senior Pilot

This rating was instituted in 1937 as "Military Airplane Pilot." The original criteria for the senior rating was at least 12 years of pilot experience with a minimum of 2000 flying hours. In 1940, the badge designation was changed from Military Airplane Pilot to Senior Pilot. During World War II the requirements were changed to 1500 hours of flying time and five years experience as a pilot.

Command Pilot

This rating was authorized on November 10, 1941 just after the Senior Pilot Badge. It is the same design as the Senior Pilot Wings but has a wreath encircling the star. Initial criteria for this rating was 15 years of flying service and 2000 flying hours. Later qualification for this rating was determined by an examination of total active service time (10, 15, 20 years), flying time (2000 or 3000 hours), and formation time.

Navigator Wings

Established on September 4, 1942, the navigator rating was awarded to graduates of the AAF aerial navigation course. The center of the wing is an armillary sphere, an ancient astronomical instrument.

Bombardier Wings

Authorized on September 4, 1942, it depicts a bomb falling on a target, the same emblem used on earlier "Annual Distinguished Bomber" Awards. To be awarded this badge, an aircrew member must have been a graduate of the AAF bombardier training program.

Enlisted Aircrew Member Wings

Authorized on Sept. 4, 1942 and initially given to various aircrew positions including gunners, flight engineers, aerial photographers, and other positions. Many AAF personnel had both enlisted aircrew member wings and their specialty wings such as gunner wings but only one pair of wings was worn. In most cases, AAF personnel who did have both wings wore their specialty wings.

Aerial Gunner Badge

Authorized on September 4, 1942, it depicts a bomb falling on a target. To be awarded this badge, an aircrew member must have been a graduate of the AAF bombardier training program. This badge could continue to be worn when the individual was no longer assigned if the crewmember was injured in enemy action or while performing duties as a member of an aircrew.

Flight Engineer Wings

Authorized on June 19, 1945, these wings were awarded to those crewmembers who performed the flight engineer function. Many flight engineers also performed other flight duties such as gunner on a bomber crew. Most AAF aircrew members who were authorized these wings usually only wore the Enlisted Aircrew Member wings. Because of the timing of the authorization of the wings at the end of World War II, many aircrew members never received or wore the flight engineer wings. The wings were worn for only about five years after they were authorized and were primarily worn by B-29 flight engineers. At the center of the wings is the front bank of nine cylinders of a stylized aircraft engine, surmounted by a four-bladed propeller.

Technical Observer Wings

Authorized on November 10, 1941, this badge was awarded to officers who were rated as a pilot or balloon pilot and who were certified by their commander as qualified to perform technical observation duty.

Liaison Pilot Wings

This badge with a "L" in the center of the wing was established on September 4, 1942 and was dropped by the AAF shortly thereafter. To obtain this rating, pilots must have flown small lightweight aircraft; their primary duty was to perform as artillery spotters in aircraft such as L-4s and L-5s. Other duties included messenger, courier, ferry, utility, and reconnaissance flights. Assignments for those qualified were restricted to liaison type aircraft of 190 horsepower. Initially, this rating could be held by both officers and enlisted men; the granting of the wings to enlisted men was eventually discontinued. There was no senior version of this rating badge.

Combat Observer (Aircraft Observer) Wings

This badge was established on October 14, 1921 and was discontinued on July 26, 1949. It was redesignated as "Aircraft Observer" on November 10, 1941. It was issued to graduates of bombardier school until Bombardier wings were introduced. It was awarded to pilots who qualified as expert or sharpshooter in aerial gunnery and who had been certified as competent in conducting aircraft observer duties; they must have also been assigned as a member of a combat crew in an air observation or reconnaissance unit and also qualifed as both a navigator and bombardier or must have been a graduate of the AAF Tactical School and have at least six years as an AAF rated pilot. The badge was awarded to bombardiers, navigators, flight engineers, radio observer night fighters, and radio observers; they were required to have completed applicable courses, demonstrated proficiency in their skill during combat missions, and to be certified proficient by their commander after having flown at least 50 hours.

Senior Aircraft Observer Wings

Awarded to individuals who had not less than 5 years' experience a Combat Observer (Aircraft Observer) and had flown at least 500 hours in that position.

Service Pilot Wings

Established on September 4, 1942, these wings with an "S" in the center of the shield were awarded to qualified pilots with previous civilian experience who were recommended by a board of officers to fly only transport, liaison, and other non-combat aircraft outside the theaters of operation; duties performed by these pilots included flying instructor, ferry pilot, transport and cargo pilot, messenger and courier service pilot, testing pilot, and tow and utility pilot. Qualification required 300 or more flying hours of which 200 must have been solo.

Senior Service Pilot Wings

Service pilots were required to have 1500 military flying hours and five years as a civilian pilot to wear these wings that bear a star above the Service Pilot wing.

Glider Pilot Wings

Established on September 4, 1942, the Glider Pilot Wing was awarded to graduates of an advanced course in glider pilot training. Pilots could obtain this rating by completing 3 hours of glider flight time, at least 10 glider landings, passing a glider flight test, and being recommended by an examining board. Glider pilots were usually in the rank of staff sergeant or flight officer. The glider badge shown under the wings is described on page 21.

Balloon Pilot Wings

This badge was awarded for completion of the balloon pilot's course in military airships or motorized balloons. It was originally authorized on January 25, 1919 as "Balloon Observer Badge." On February 20, 1940, it was redesignated as "Balloon Pilot." To be awarded the badge, an individual must have had five years as a rated balloon pilot and have flown at least 100 hours as a pilot in military airships or military motorized balloons.

Senior Balloon Pilot Wings

This rating was awarded to balloon pilots who had attained at least 1000 hours of airship or motorized balloon flying and ten years' service in air units. It is the same design as the Balloon Pilot Badge except it has a star centered above the balloon. It was authorized on November 10, 1941.

Balloon Observer Wings

Balloon observer wings were authorized in 1940 when the original "ballon observer" wings became "balloon pilot" wings. The wings were awarded to balloon pilots who were qualified as a sharpshooter or expert aerial gunner, were certified by their commander as competent for conducting balloon observer duties, and were either assigned as a certified aircraft observer while a member of a combat crew in a balloon unit or a graduate of the AAF Tactical School having at least six years as an AAF rated pilot.

Airship Pilot Wings

This badge was authorized in 1919 and was awarded to graduates of the Air Corps Balloon and Airship School who had not less than 200 hours of flying time and had at least 75 hours of solo time. This rating was abolished on February 20, 1940. Less than a hundred officers were authorized to wear the badge that featured a dirigible in the center of the oxidized silver wings.

Women's Air Force Service Pilots (WASP) Wings

These wings became the official wings presented to graduates of the WASP school from 1943 onward. Initially, wings with training class numbers imprinted on the shields were presented prior to this wing becoming the official wing for the WASP. The regulation WASP wings were smaller than regulation pilot wings and were similar to pilot wings except the shield was replaced with a lozenge design. The lozenge design represents the shield of Athena, goddess of war, and also a heraldic symbol used for unmarried women or widows.

Flight Surgeon Wings

The flight surgeon rating was introduced in 1942, and was officially authorized in 1943 for the AAF. To be awarded these wings in the AAF, the individual must have been a civilian physician who was qualified as an aviation medical examiner; one year of military service and 50 hours of flying time were also required. The wings were initially gold in color and were changed to silver on September 12, 1944. The wing has the caduceus centered on the circular design in the center of the wing.

Flight Nurse Wings

Flight nurse wings were established on December 15, 1943 and were awarded to women in the Army Nurse Corps who served at least six months in an AAF hospital and who completed an eight week training course approved by the Commanding General, AAF. Nurses served on board casualty evacuation aircraft such as the C-47 "Gooney Bird." The original wings were gold but were changed to silver on September 12, 1944 and had an "N" in the center of the caduceus in the center of the wing. The "N" could have been maroon with a silver edge or just silver. The wings were made only in a two inch size.

United States Air Force (USAF) Wings

To be a "rated" officer in the USAF, a commissioned officer must complete prescribed USAF training, or one designated as equivalent by Headquarters USAF. The only flying positions that qualify as "rated" are pilot, navigator/observer, and flight surgeon. Ratings are awarded by publication of an aeronautical order; this order constitutes the authority to wear the associated aviation badge. Total rated service is calculated from the date the officer is awarded the basic USAF rating. Advanced ratings are/have been awarded primarily on the basis of total flying time and total rated service time. The criteria for award of advanced ratings has changed several times; in some cases, past criteria is included along with present day criteria.

Pilot Wings

The individual must be a commissioned officer and must be a graduate of USAF Undergraduate Pilot Training (UPT) or a graduate of pilot or helicopter training conducted by another military service, provided that training is equivalent to USAF training; the individual must also be physically qualified by in accordance with current regulations.

Senior Pilot

A pilot must have at least seven years rated status to qualify for this wing; other requirements include 2000 flying hours or 1300 hours of instructor/first pilot time and 72 months of operational flying experience by the 12th year of aviation service. The star centered 1/16th inch above the wing is 1/2 inch in diameter.

Command Pilot

Qualification for this rating badge was initially determined by an examination of total active service time (10, 15, 20 years), flying time (2000 or 3000 hours), and formation time. In the USAF, the requirement was to have at least 15 years rated service, 3000 hours as a pilot (or 2300 hours of first pilot/instructor pilot time), and 132 months of operational flying experience by the 18th year of aviation service.

Navigator or Aircraft Observer

The "nav" wing contains a USAF Seal in the center of the shield. To be awarded this rating, the individual must be a commissioned officer and must have completed prescribed USAF training or one designated as equivalent by HQ USAF (currently must be a graduate of Undergraduate Navigator Training (UNT), USAF Specialized Navigator Training (SUNT), or the U.S. Naval Observer Course. Observer ratings are approved by HQ USAF and denote professional qualifications resulting from training in a flying specialty other than pilot or navigator.

Senior Navigator or Senior Aircraft Observer

The senior navigator rating was initially awarded for 6 years operational experience as a navigator. USAF regulations in 1958 specified that both written and flight examinations were required to be awarded this rating. Regulations later required 7 years rated status as a navigator, 2000 total flight hours (1300 hours if 1000 hours was jet time), and 72 months of operational flying experience by the 12th year of aviation service. It has a five-pointed star centered above the wing.

Master Navigator or Master Aircraft Observer

The master navigator rating was initially awarded for 15 years operational experience as a navigator. Regulations later required 15 years rated status as a navigator, 3000 total flight hours (2300 hours if at least 2000 were jet time), and 132 months of operational flying experience by the 18th year of aviation service. It has a wreath of silver oak leaves encircling a five-pointed star above the shield.

Nonrated Officer Aircrew Member

     This wing is awarded to a non-rated officer (NRO) who is assigned to and performing a designated aircrew duty. The United States Coat of Arms is contained within a shield in the center of the wing.

Senior Nonrated Officer Aircrew Member

     This senior badge is awarded for 7 years service and 60 months as an aircrew member. A star rests above the U.S. Coat of Arms.

Chief Nonrated Officer Aircrew Member

     A non-rated officer aircrew member must have 15 years service and 120 months as an aircrew member to be awarded this badge. A star encircled by a wreath rests above the U.S. Coat of Arms.

Flight Surgeon

     The staff of Aesculapius, the symbol of medicine, is in the center of the shield in the center of the wing. The individual must be an officer graduate of the Aerospace Medicine Primary Course or a graduate of similar training conducted by another military service; the doctor must be trained to take care of health concerns of aircrew members.

Senior Flight Surgeon

     Requirements for the senior flight surgeon badge were 7 years total service and 350 flying hours logged as a flight surgeon. Wing has the standard star centered above the wing.

Chief Flight Surgeon

     This badge was awarded after 15 years of total service and at least 750 flying hours logged as a flight surgeon. A star sits atop the wing against a silver scroll.

Flight Nurse (USAF)

     Awardees must have completed the appropriate course at the USAF School of Aerospace Medicine. Wing design has Aesculapius' staff superimposed over Florence Nightingale's lamp. It is available in only the two inch size. *NOW FULLSIZE.*

Senior Flight Nurse

     Flight nurses must have completed 7 years of total service, 5 years as a flight nurse, and at least 750 hours of patient time to qualify for this badge. Later requirements mandated 36 months of aircrew duty as a flight nurse and at least 7 years of total military service with 500 hours logged as a flight nurse. It has the star centered atop the basic Flight Nurse wing.

Chief Flight Nurse

Early requirements said that senior flight nurses could earn this badge by completing 15 years of total service and 500 hours of patient time. Later requirements were 72 months aircrew duty as a flight nurse and at least 15 years of total military service with 1000 hours logged as a flight nurse. A star sits atop the wing against a silver scroll.

Astronaut Wings

Astronaut wings have the astronaut symbol (shooting star symbol) superimposed over the the particular specialty wing such as pilot, navigator, flight surgeon, etc. They are awarded to USAF rated officers who are qualified to perform duties in their respective rating in space (50 miles or more above the earth) and have completed a minimum of one operational space mission. Pilot, navigator, and flight surgeon wings are shown to demonstrate how the wings are constructed. Senior and command pilot badge requirements are the same as for other senior and chief astronaut badges.

Pilot Astronaut

The astronaut symbol (the shooting star) is superimposed on the pilot shield in the center of the wing. The wing is authorized for pilots who have made at least one flight more than 50 miles from the earth.

Senior Pilot Astronaut

This badge has the five pointed star centered above the wing. The individual must have been rated as a senior pilot prior to participating in flight above 50 miles altitude.

Command Pilot Astronaut

The star above the wings is encircled by a wreath of oak leaves. The individual must have been rated as a command pilot before participating in a flight above 50 miles altitude.

Enlisted Aircrew Member

The enlisted aircrew member wing for the USAF is the same as that of the AAF which was established on September 4, 1942 and was initially given to various aircrew positions including gunners, flight engineers, aerial photographers, and other positions. Later regulations specified that enlisted personnel must be assigned to an aircrew operations career field to qualify for this badge. Unlike the AAF, enlisted personnel in the USAF today wear this badge only. Until after the Korean War, enlisted personnel often still wore their specialty badge, such as flight engineer and gunner badge. The badge is a wing that has the United States Coat of Arms in the center.

SENIOR ENLISTED AIRCREW MEMBER

This wing is awarded to enlisted personnel who have 7 years service and 60 months as an enlisted aircrew member. Airmen must have held a 5-level skill rating as a crewmember. It has the star centered above the wing.

CHIEF ENLISTED AIRCREW MEMBER

Requirements for this badge are 15 years enlisted service and 120 months as an enlisted aircrew member. Airmen must have held a 7-level skill rating as a crewmember. It has a wreath encircling a star centered above the wing.

United States Air Force Insignia

Bandsman Hat Device

Members of the U.S. Air Force Band wear a distinctive hat badge consisting of a lyre, an ancient Greek stringed instrument, superimposed upon an aircrew style wing badge that has a propeller mounted vertically through the center .

Officer Cap Device

The USAF officer cap device is the emblem of the United States Coat of Arms. As of October 1, 1997, only majors and above are required to wear the service cap. The men's device measures vertically 2 3/8" while the women's cap device measures 1 5/8".

U.S. Lapel Insignia

The officer USAF "US" insignia is silver-colored metal 7/16" in height with beveled edges. The enlisted USAF insignia, prior to June 1, 1995, had the "U.S." within a beveled ring one inch in diameter. In 1995, the enlisted circular insignia was eliminated; both officer and enlisted now wear the same highly polished "US" insignia on the service dress uniform..

Enlisted Cap Device

As of this date, the enlisted service cap is no longer authorized and worn by enlisted personnel. The cap insignia that had been used previously has the United States coat of arms within a circular ring. The hat insignia measures 1 11/16 inches in diameter.

Chief Master Sgt. of the Air Force Lapel Insignia

A wreath, symbol of excellence, surrounds the "U.S." to provide a distinctive collar insignia for the uniform of the Chief Master Sergeant of the Air Force. The insignia is 1 and 1/8 inch in diameter.

Chief Master Sgt. of the Air Force Cap Device

A wreath, symbol of excellence, surrounds the U.S. coat of arms to provide a distinctive cap insignia for the Chief Master Sergeant of the Air Force.

Band Lapel Insignia

Members of the U.S. Air Force Band wear a distinctive collar insignia which represents a lyre, a harplike ancient Greek instrument.

Aide Insignia

Officers assigned as aides are distinguished by silver-color aiguillettes which are worn on the left shoulder of the service or dress uniform except for presidential aides who wear their's on the right shoulder. Aides are also distinguished by metal insignia which denotes the office or rank of the commander to which they are assigned. The eleven different aide insignia are shown below.

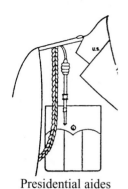
Presidential aides

Female Officer aides   Officers aides

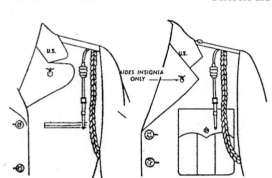

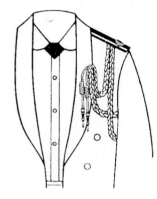 
Officers aides formal attire

Aide to Brig. General

Aide to Major General   Aide to Lt. General   Aide to General   Air Aide to General of USAF   Aide to Chief of Staff

Aide to Chairman Joint Chiefs of Staff   Aide to Secretary of the Air Force   Aide to Secretary of Defense   Aide to Vice-President of the United States   Aide to President of the United States

Occupational Badges

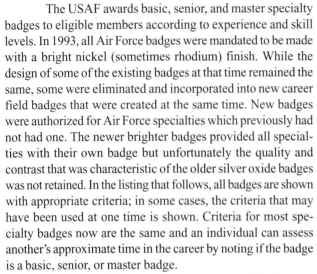

The USAF awards basic, senior, and master specialty badges to eligible members according to experience and skill levels. In 1993, all Air Force badges were mandated to be made with a bright nickel (sometimes rhodium) finish. While the design of some of the existing badges at that time remained the same, some were eliminated and incorporated into new career field badges that were created at the same time. New badges were authorized for Air Force specialties which previously had not had one. The newer brighter badges provided all specialties with their own badge but unfortunately the quality and contrast that was characteristic of the older silver oxide badges was not retained. In the listing that follows, all badges are shown with appropriate criteria; in some cases, the criteria that may have been used at one time is shown. Criteria for most specialty badges now are the same and an individual can assess another's approximate time in the career by noting if the badge is a basic, senior, or master badge.

Many of the advanced occupational badges are currently awarded according to accumulated time in that specialty. Enlisted personnel must complete initial skill training or possess a 5-level Air Force specialty code to wear any of the basic specialty badges. Current requirements specify that officers may wear the basic badge after graduating from technical school (or after attaining a fully qualified AFSC if technical school is not required). To be eligible for the senior badge enlisted members must have a 7-level AFSC and officers must have fully qualified AFSCs and 7 years' experience. Current requirements for the master badge mandate 5 years in the specialty from award of the 7-skill level and a rank of master sergeant or above for enlisted personnel while officers could wear the master badge after 15 years in the specialty. Medical Service officers may have constructive service credit for civilian experience/education that may affect their eligibility for award of their respective career field badges. Occupational badges are 1 5/8 inches in width while medical style badges are 11/16 in height and 5/8 in width.

Occupational badges are grouped by current regulations into specific career areas as denoted below. A discussion of "missile " badges precedes the listing of the specific career groups since missile badges have the distinction of being one of the most misunderstood Air Force badges. The original missile badge should be grouped in the operations career area while that same badge today is grouped under the logistics area since it is now a "missile maintenance badge."

MISSILEMAN/MISSILE BADGE

According to AFR 35-5, dated May 23, 1958, Guided Missile Insignia was awarded to officers and airmen who possessed a guided missile AFSC or performed a direct, distinctive role in the command, maintenance, or operation of the missile or its aerospace ground equipment (AGE). Authorization to wear "guided missile insignia" included:

1. Personnel had to be assigned to a guided missile unit or a staff position in that field.

2. Airmen must have a 5 level (skilled) in their career field.

3. Officers and airmen must have satisfactorily demonstrated their ability for at least three months.

4. Personnel must be recommended by their immediate supervisor.

5. Personnel could also be assigned to research and development, testing, planning, or logistics with a primary duty directly associated with guided missiles.

6. Personnel must be assigned with one of the following weapon systems: Snark, Atlas, Titan, Goose, Thor, Jupiter, Matador, Mace, Bomarc, or Minuteman.

That same regulation in 1963 changed the name of the "Guided Missile Insignia" to the "Missileman Badge " and also established a basic, senior and master badge. The senior missileman badge required 3 years of satisfactory performance in the missile duty position and the master missileman badge required 7 years of satisfactory performance in the missile duty position.

Specific requirements to be awarded the badge have varied since its inception. The initial requirement for formalized training was deleted in 1974 thus broadening the range of eligibility to just about anyone who had anything to do with the missile field. In 1979, the badge name was changed from Missileman Badge to Missile Badge. In 1984, the creation of the Space Badge and the Aircraft Munitions/Maintenance Badge removed the Missile Badge from many previously eligible personnel. At that same time, the time in duty positon requirement was extended to 5 years for the senior badge and 10 years for the master badge and a tour of duty in a guided missile unit became mandatory for award of the advanced level badges. That same year, the badge became a temporary award that would become permanent if the recipient completed two years of qualifying service. In 1985 the time requirement for the senior badge was changed back to 3 years and the advanced badge criteria was kept at 10 years. In 1988 the senior badge time requirement was changed to 4 years while the master badge requirement remained at 10 years. In 1993, the criteria changed to 3 and 4 years, respectively, for the senior and master badges and the award became permanent after it had been earned with no specific minimum time requirement in a missile duty position.

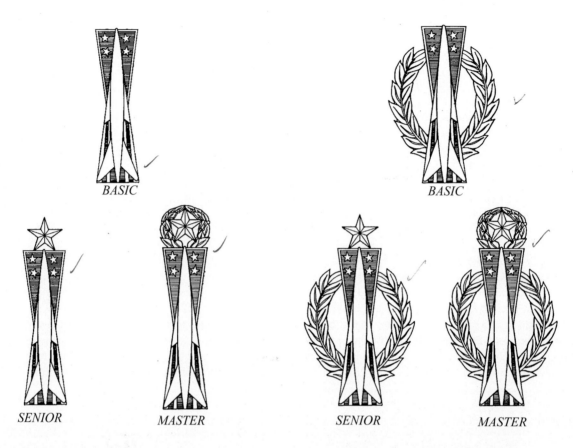

Basic Missile/Missile Maintenance Badge

Awarded to both officers and enlisted personnel whose primary job was with missile operations/missile support activities. In 1996, this badge became the Missile Maintenance Badge and is awarded to predominantly missile personnel who support missile operations through maintenance activities.

Senior Missile/Missile Maintenance Badge

Officers must be eligible for the Basic Missile Badge and have satisfactorily performed duty in the missile career field for 48 months

Master (Command) Missile/Missile Maintenance Badge

Officers must be eligibile for the Basic and Senior Missile Badge and have satisfactorily performed duty in their assigned missile career field for at least 120 months.

Missile Operator/Missile Badge

The Missile Operator Badge was established in 1988 for personnel involved solely in missile operations. It was originally called the "Missile Operator Badge". The large wreath on either side of the old style badge was called the "Operations Designator." The official name became "Missile Badge with Operations Designator." It is awarded to officers after graduation from missile school at Vandenburg AFB and upon qualification as a missile combat crew member.

Senior Missile Operator/Senior Missile Badge

The Senior Missile Operator Badge is awarded after three years of operational time as a missile operator. At one time, its official name was "Senior Missile Badge with Operations Designator."

Master Missile Operator/Master Missile Badge

The Master Missile Operator Badge is awarded after ten years of operational time as a missile operator. At one time, its official name was "Command Missile Badge."

Operations Support Badge

Authorized in 1993 for officers and enlisted personnel in the operations support career field. Duties involved in this career field include: international affairs; dealing with foreign governments; international technology transfer and security controls; international personal exchange support; arms control agreements; and strategic arms reduction treaty tracking and reporting. The badge is authorized also for safety officers and enlisted personnel in safety, survival training, life aircrew support, and pararescue career fields.

Air Traffic Controller Badge

Awarded to officer and enlisted personnel in the applicable AFSC who are graduates of a formal DOD/FAA Air Traffic Controller (ATC) course and possess a valid ATC certificate. The training and job assignment ot these personnel enables them to have a direct and distinct role in the control of air traffic in support of the Air Force mission. The senior badge required a minimum of 7 years and the master badge required a minimum of 15 years of practical ATC experience. This badge was replaced by the Command and Control Badge and will be obsolete in 1998.

Weapons Controller Badge

Awarded to officers and enlisted personnel who have a direct role in the command and control, management, and direction of air operations. Awardee must have completed USAF Air Weapons Controller School or a HQ USAF recognized air weapons controller system qualification course; if individual did not attend the listed courses, they could receive the badge after assignment to an operational unit and upon initial upgrade or after assignment to a staff level position for 12 months. The senior badge required a total of 3 years in position and the master badge required a total of 7 years in position. This badge will be obsolete in 1998 and has been replaced by the Command and Control Badge.

Command and Control Badge

Authorized in 1993 and awarded to officers in the command and control operations field and to enlisted personnel in the command and control sytems operations career field. This field now incorporates the weapons controller and air traffic controller career fields which previously had their own badges. Other functions included in this career field are ground radar systems; tactical air control party; airspace management; air support operations; rescue coordination; and the deployment of airfield operations.

Space/Missile Badge

Originally authorized as the Space Badge in 1982 and in 1993 was renamed the Space and Missile Badge. It was intended to replace the missile badge which was prohibited for wear after October 1998; this prohibition never went into effect since the regulation was rescinded in 1995. The space/missile badge is awarded to officers in the astronaut and space and missile operations career field and to enlisted personnel in the space systems career field. Individuals must have performed in a space duty position in a space unit for 12 months to receive the basic space badge. Missileers receive the badge after graduating from the Undergraduate Space and Missile Training at Vandenberg AFB, California and are currently authorized to wear both this badge and the appropriate missile badge "pocket rocket."

Meteorologist Badge

Authorized in 1987, the basic badge was awarded to officers who possess a fully qualified AFSC and one year of experience in the career field and to enlisted personnel who held a 5-level AFSC in the weather career area. To obtain the senior badge, officers had to have seven years' experience and a fully qualified AFSC while enlisted personnel needed a 7-level AFSC. The master badge required officers to hold a staff-level position and to have 12 years of experience while enlisted personnel were required to hold a 9-level AFSC. In 1993 along with all other specialty badges, the criteria for award of the senior and master badges was changed to three and seven years, respectively. The badge design was retained but was made with the newer bright finish.

Intelligence Badge

Authorized in 1993 and awarded to both officers and enlisted personnel in the intelligence career field. Intelligence duties include: the collection, production, and application of intelligence information; threat recognition training; producing cartographic materials; gathering inputs and information for targeting; and the control, protection, and dissemination of sensitive intelligence information.

Communications-Electronics Maintenance Badge

This badge was authorized in 1987 and awarded to eligible members according to skill levels and experience. Officers must have a fully qualified AFSC and one year of experience in the communications-computer systems career field and enlisted personnel must possess a 5-level AFSC in one of the communications-electronics or wire communications systems maintenance specialties to qualify for the basic badge. For the senior badge, officers must be fully qualified in their AFSC with 7 years experience while enlisted personnel must have a 7-level in their AFSC. The master badge requires officers to have 12 years' experience and to hold a staff-level position while enlisted personnel must have a 9-level AFSC. This badge will be obsolete in 1998 and has already been replaced with the Maintenance Badge which was authorized in 1993.

Transportation Badge

Authorized in 1993 and awarded to officers in the transportation career field and to enlisted personnel in the marine transportation and vehicle maintenance career fields.

Logistics Badge

Authorized in 1993 and awarded to officers in the logistics plans and programs career field and to enlisted personnel in the logistics plans career field.

Supply-Fuels Badge (Old & New)

Authorized in 1987 for eligible officers and enlisted personnel according to skill levels and experience. Officers must have a specialty in the supply management career area

and one year of experience while enlisted personnel must hold a 5-level AFSC in the fuels or supply career fields to qualify for the basic badge. To qualify for the senior badge, officers must have a fully qualified AFSC and seven years' experience and enlisted personnel need a 7-level AFSC. The master badge requires officers to be in a staff level position and have 12 years' experience and enlisted personnel to hold a 9-level AFSC.

older design

This badge has already been replaced by the new design Supply-Fuels Specialty Badge and will be obsolete in 1998. The new bright finish badge design is quite different from the older design; in the new design, the eagle's wings are folded and in the old design, they are open, pointed upward. The advanced badges are awarded based on the new criteria of three and seven years' experience for the senior and master badges, respectively. On the color plate, an old style basic supply-fuels badge is shown along with a new style master supply-fuels badge. (Note the difference in definition between the older style and the new stay bright style.)

Aircraft and Munitions Maintenance Badge

Awarded to officers and enlisted personnel who hold AFSC's in the aircraft and munitions maintenance areas. This badge is the same design as the newer Maintenance badge but has the duller finish; it will be obsolete in 1998.

Maintenance Badge

Authorized in 1993 and awarded to officers in aircraft maintenance/munitions and space/missile maintenance career fields. Individuals must have completed a technical school in a designated maintenance specialty. This badge replaced the aircraft and munitions maintenance badge, the missile maintenance badge, and the communications-electronics maintenance badge which will be obsolete in 1998.

Civil Engineer Badge

Authorized in 1993 and awarded to officers and enlisted personnel in the civil engineer field. Individuals in this career field who are also qualified in the EOD (Explosive Ordnance Disposal) career field may wear the appropriate EOD badge. Some of the duties incorporated into this field include: power plant management; construction of roads, buildings and airfields; fire protection; base housing; disaster preparedness; hazardous material management and disposal; environmental protection; real estate; and explosive ordnance disposal.

Band Badge

Authorized in 1993 and awarded to both officers and enlisted personnel in the band career field. The Air Force Band was created in 1941 as the Bolling Army Air Corps Band. The purpose of the Air Force bands is to maintain troop morale and to aid USAF retention and recruiting programs. There are two premiere bands -- the USAF Band and the USAF Band of the Rockies. There are nine regional bands in the U.S. and three bands in overseas locations. The USAF Band consists of several instrumental and singing groups that perform all over the world to a variety of audiences in a variety of settings. These groups include: The Singing Sergeants; The Airmen of Note; the Concert Band; High Flight; Silver Wings; The Strolling Strings; Ceremonial Brass; and the Chamber Players.

Communications Badge

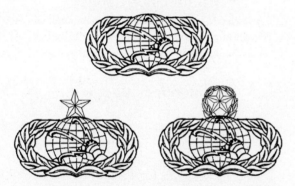

Authorized in 1993 and awarded to both officers and enlisted personnel in the communications-computer systems career field and to enlisted personnel in the visual information career field. In 1997, the communications career field merged with the information management career field. The badge design did not change. Some of the duties incorporated into this career field include: communications security; radio, telephones, and the Military Affiliate Radio System (MARS); data administration and software management; and cryptosystems.

Services Badge

Authorized in 1993 and awarded to both officers and enlisted personnel in the services career field and to enlisted personnel in the commissary services career field. Some of the duties and responsibilities that are incorporated in this career field include: morale, welfare, and recreation programs; fitness and sports programs; library services; aero clubs; mortuary affairs; food services; laundry services; the honor guard program; and youth programs.

Public Affairs Badge

Authorized in 1993 and awarded to both officers and enlisted personel in the public affairs career field. Responsibilities included in the public affairs career field include: the Air Force Band; community relations; media relations; base newspapers; and the Armed Forces Radio and Television Service.

Historian Badge

Authorized in 1993 and awarded to only enlisted personnel in the historian career field. This career field has the responsibility of gathering and organizing unit historical information including artistic works in order to preserve the heritage of the associated base, unit , or major command. In light of the numerous base closings and unit inactivations, this field has become even more important over the last several years. The career field also has the responsibility of coordinating with the Air Force museum system to insure proper disposal of historical items.

Manpower and Personnel Badge

Authorized in 1993 and awarded to officers assigned as chief, mission support or to the personnel or manpower career fields and to enlisted personnel assigned to mission support or manpower career fields.

Administration (Information Management) Badge (old & new)

Initially authorized in 1987, this badge was awarded to officers and enlisted personnel who held AFSCs in the administration career area. Officers must have possessed a fully qualified AFSC and one year of experience in the career field to be awarded the basic badge while enlisted personnel required a 5-level AFSC. Senior badges required officers to have seven years' experience and enlisted personnel to have a 7-level AFSC. For the master badge, officers needed to have a staff-level position and 12 years' experience and enlisted personnel needed a 9-level AFSC. This badge has already been replaced by the new Information Management Badge and will be obsolete in 1998. Requirements for the new badge changed to correspond with the other badges that were created - three and seven years' experience for senior and master badges, respectively. In 1997, this career field merged with the communications career field. Personnel will wear both badges until upgrading to the senior or master level when they will then wear the new badge.

Security Police Qualification Badge

Awarded to officers and enlisted personnel who have attained required levels of skill and demonstrated prolonged honorable service in the security police career field. Officers must have completed the basic security police officer course or the staff officer course and have a minimum of 6 months continuous or cumulative service in the security police career field. Enlisted personnel must have completed the basic security police school and have a minimum of 6 months of continuous/cumulative service in the security police career field. The basic badge entailed a probationary period of one year. The senior badge required a minimum of 7 years of continuous/cumulative service and the master badge required a minimum of 15 years in the security police AFSC. The above criteria for the master badge did not apply to personnel assigned as the USAF Chief of Security Police or as a MAJCOM (Major Command) Chief of Security Police; the master badge was withdrawn upon termination of assignment in the mentioned positions. This badge did not replace the Security Police Identification Badge.

Judge Advocate Badge

Awarded to officers designated as judge advocates and also to legal officers of the Air National Guard. They must be professionally qualified — i.e. graduate of law school accredited by the American Bar Association and admitted to practice law before the highest court of a State or Federal Court. The badge identifies Air Force officers who are designated to perform legal functions for the Air Force and its personnel. All new judge advocate generals are required to attend the Judge Advocate Staff Officer Course at the Air Force Judge Advocate General School at Maxwell AFB, Alabama. The Badge is 1 1/8 " in width and 3/4 " in height. The badge was approved for wear in 1967. The design of the insignia reflects the logo of the Air Force JAG Law Review.

Law Enforcement Badge

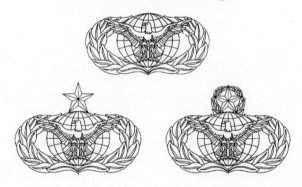

Awarded to both officers and enlisted personnel assigned to either the security police or the special investigations career fields. Replaces the security police qualification badge which becomes obsolete in 1998. The law enforcement career field is responsible for providing security for personnel and resources, enforcing both federal, military, and state laws, maintaining the installation correction facility, conducting investigations, and maintaining an effective anti-terrorism program.

Paralegal Badge

Awarded to enlisted personnel only who are assigned to the paralegal career field after completion of the paralegal course at the Air Force Judge Advocate General School at Maxwell AFB, Alabama. Design was taken from the Judge Advocate Badge. The scales of justice represent the military legal system and the quills represent the support given by the paralegal force.

Chaplain Badge (Christian, Jewish, Buddhist, Muslim)

Awarded to officers who are assigned as chaplains. Officers wearing a chaplain badge should be referred to as "Chaplain" regardless of rank. The Chaplain Cross identifies the officer wearing it as a Christian chaplain, which includes Protestants, Catholics, and Orthodox faith groups. The Chaplain Tablet is worn by Jewish chaplains and consists of two tablets of the Ten Commandments surmounted by a six-pointed Star of David. The tablets are overlaid with Hebrew letters numbering one through ten. The Buddhist Chaplain badge is representative of the Buddhist "wheel of life" which shows the different stages that one will progress through in their religious development. The Muslim Chaplain badge is designed to represent the Islamic Crescent, the symbol for Islamic followers. The first Muslim chaplain candidate was commissioned in January 1997; upon qualification, he will be the first active-duty Muslim chaplain for the Air Force.

Chaplain Service Support

Awarded to enlisted personnel only who are assigned to the chaplain service support career field. These personnel are non-clergy members of the Air Force Chaplain Service and manage support of Air Force chaplain activities.

Acquisition and Financial Management Career Group
Acquisition and Financial Management Badge

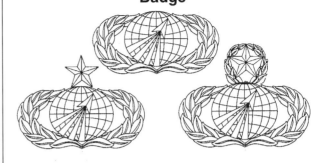

Awarded to officers in the scientific/research developmental engineering, acquisition, contracting, and financial management career fields. Awarded to enlisted personnel in the contracting and financial management career fields.

Explosive Ordnance Disposal (EOD) Badge

The basic EOD badge is awarded to officers and enlisted members who have completed the basic EOD course taught at the US Naval EOD School, Indian Head, Maryland and are assigned to a position for which the course is a prerequisite. Initial screening for USAF personnel is done at Lackland AFB, Texas. USAF personnel attend a "pre-EOD School" Navy course at Eglin AFB, Florida. Personnel must serve in the position for a period of 18 months for the award to be permanent. The wreath on the badge symbolizes the achievements and laurels gained by EOD personnel. The bomb design is copied from the design of the World War II Bomb Disposal Badge and its three fins represent the major areas of nuclear, conventional, and chemical/biological interests. The lightning bolts symbolize the potential destructive power and the courage and professionalism of the EOD personnel. The shield represents the EOD mission to prevent a detonation and to protect personnel and property.

The Senior Explosive Ordnance Badge is awarded to personnel who have served in an EOD position for at least 36 months. Current regulations specify the individual must be a staff sergeant with a 7-level in the EOD AFSC. The Master EOD Badge is awarded to personnel who have been awarded the Senior EOD Badge, have sixty months of cumulative service in an EOD position, and have been recommended by their immediate commander. Current requirements for the master badge specify proficiency of at least 10 years after graduation from the Basic School and for enlisted personnel a 9-level in the EOD AFSC and the rank of master sergeant.

Medical Corps Badges

Awarded to officers who are assigned to the medical career field as physicians. The criteria for the basic badge is graduation from Medical School (physicians in residency programs are therefore authorized to wear the badge). To wear the senior physician badge, the doctor must complete a residency in a specialty field such as surgery, pediatrics, etc. to become "board eligible." Once a physician becomes board certified in a specialty recognized by the American Board of Medical Specialties, the individual may wear the chief medical corps badge.

Medical Service Corps (MSC) Badge

Awarded to officers who are assigned to the health service administrator career field and who have attended the Health Services Administration Course at Sheppard AFB, Texas. Badge is awarded upon commissioning as an MSC officer.

Biomedical Science Corps (BSC) Badge

Awarded to officers who are assigned as biomedical science officers. All specialities in the BSC career field require an appropriate level degree as specified by Air Force regulations and receive approval by the USAF Surgeon General. Specialities included in the BSC field are bioenviromental engineer, aerospace physiologist, biomedical laboratory officer, biomedical specialist, chiropractor, clinical psychologist, clinical social worker, dietitian, health physicist, medical entomologist, occupational therapist, pharmacist, physician assistant, physical therapist, podiatrist, and public health officer.

Nurse Corps Badge

Awarded to officers assigned to the USAF Nurse Corps. The original nurse corps badge was approved in 1972.

To be awarded the senior nurse badge at that time required that a nurse possess a doctoral degree and have 5 years nursing experience; a masters degree with 7 years experience; a baccalaureate degree with 10 years experience; or 13 years military nursing service. The chief nurse badge required a doctoral degree with 10 years nursing experience; a masters degree with 13 years experience; a baccalaureate degree with 16 years experience and selection by a board of officers appointed by the USAF Surgeon General; or 19 years of nursing experience and selection by a board of officers also appointed by the USAF Surgeon General. Current regulations state that applicants must have successfully passed the National Council Licensure Examination for Registered Nurses and must possess a current registration in at least one state, in a U.S. territory, Puerto Rico, or the District of Columbia. Current requirements for advanced badges are like all other medical badges, 3 and 7 years experience, respectively.

Dental Corps Badge

Awarded to officers assigned to the USAF Dental Corps. Air Force dentists must possess a dental degree from a school accredited by the American Dental Association. Previous qualifications required residency completion for the senior dental corps badge and board certification for the chief dental corps badge. Current requirements for advanced badges are 3 and 7 years, respectively, for the senior and chief dental corps badges.

Veterinary Badge

Once a licensed veterinarian was commissioned, he/she was authorized to wear the veterinary badge. Veterinarians currently in the USAF are assigned to the Biomedical Service Corps (BSC) and as such wear the BSC badge; other veterinarian requirements for the Air Force are supported by U.S. Army veterinarians who may be assigned to the Air Force base.

Enlisted Medical Badge

Awarded to enlisted personnel assigned to the enlisted medical service member career field. This badge is identical to the **Medical Technician Badge** which is shown on the color plate except that it has the bright finish.

Special Qualification Badges

Parachutist Badge

Parachute Badge (AAF and current style)

To be awarded this badge during the AAF period, individuals had to complete proficiency tests while assigned to an airborne unit or the airborne school; or they had to participate in at least one combat parachute jump into enemy held territory. Individuals must have completed the Army Infantry School course at Fort Benning, Georgia, or a formal course taught by the Parachute Branch at the U. S. Air Force Academy.

Senior Parachutist Badge

To receive an advanced rating, parachutists must be on jump status for a specified length of time and accomplish a certain number of jumps. The **senior parachutist badge** requires a minimum of 24 months on jump status in a unit with a jump mission. The applicant must have at least 30 jumps of which two jumps must be at night, fifteen must be with prescribed equipment, and two must end in an airborne assault (real or training) (four test jumps with experimental equipment will also satisfy this requirement). The 30 jumps must also include seven jumps as a primary jumpmaster and one night deployment as a primary jumpmaster.

Master Parachutist Badge

The **master parachutist badge** requires 36 months of jump status and 65 jumps of which four must be at night, 25 must be with prescribed equipment, and five must be airborne assaults (or ten test jumps). Two jumps of the 65 must be during a night deployment while acting in the position of primary jumpmaster and fifteen jumps must be accomplished while performing as primary jumpmaster.

Parachute Badge (1956 TO 1963)

The Air Force decided in 1956 to have its own distinctive parachute badge after previously using the Army parachute badge. The badges were designed in the shield style of the USAF medical badges and had a white open parachute against a blue and white background. The senior badge bore a star centered atop the badge while the master badge has a star centered on a silver scroll above the shield. Qualifications for the badges were the same as for the Army parachute badges. The Air Force discontinued the badges in 1963 and reverted back to the Army parachutists badges. See page 128 for more detail.

Combat Crewmember Badge

The Combat Crewmember Badge was established on Sep 1, 1964. It is rectangular, 3" by 3/4", made of oxidized sterling silver. It has the Air Force Coat of Arms and the words "Combat Crew" on the face. The badge is only worn by personnel serving in positions in which they accrue creditable service toward award of the Combat Readiness Medal. Commanders certify eligibility for the badge after reviewing the organization's record of eligibility; the information is not entered on the individual's personnel record since the badge is not awarded permanently. Once a crewmember is reassigned from a combat status, the person's authority to wear the badge is terminated.

Combat Control Badge

Awarded to personnel qualified as Combat Controllers (i.e. hold an appropriate Primary, Control, or Duty AFSC). The Combat Controller career field was created in 1953 at Donaldson AFB, South Carolina to provide highly trained personnel to provide control, navigational, and guidance communications to airborne aircrews and their controlling authorities in hostile environments by both overt and covert techniques.

TACP (Tactical Air Control Party) Badge

Awarded to personnel who have satisfied the requirements to become members of a Tactical Air Control Party team which consists of both Tactical Air Command and Control Specialists and Air Liaison Officers. The badge is worn on a distinctive black beret. The mission of the TACP is to advise and assist U.S. Army ground combat commanders on the use of USAF combat air power. TACPs operate in a battlefield environment while deployed with Army units.

Pararescue Badge

Awarded to enlisted personnel who have satisfied the prerequisites for and are performing duty in the pararescue career field. The badge is worn on a distinctive maroon beret which was approved for wear in 1966 by USAF Chief of Staff, Gen. John P. McConnell. The color of the beret symbolizes the blood sacrificed by pararescuemen who are a highly trained rescue force prepared to save lives under the most intense and dangerous conditions.

Security Police Identification Badge

Issued to all qualified security police personnel performing duty in the security police career field. The badge is very distinctive from other Air Force badges to enable the individual to be readily identified as a security policeman. It is worn when in uniform while performing security and law enforcement duties, including staff duties in these areas. The security police qualification badge does not replace this badge. Men wear the badge on the left breast pocket while women wear the badge above the top row of ribbons or in the same relative position without ribbons. Original badges similar to this design had the words "Air Police" as they were first called until their name was changed to "Security Police."

Air Training Command (ATC) Instructor Badge/Air Education and Training Command (AETC) Instructor Badge

The ATC/AETC Instructor Badge identifies instructors assigned to technical training schools or programs that provide education and training. To qualify for the badge, the individual's primary duty assignment must be as an instructor; to be an instructor, the individual must complete instructor training requirements which includes a teaching practicum. If the individual is no longer assigned to a training organization, he/she can no longer wear the badge.

Air Training Command (ATC) Master Instructor Badge/Air Education and Training Command (AETC) Master Instructor Badge

To qualify for the ATC/AETC Master Instructor Badge, an instructor must serve two years as a technical training instructor, have an associate or higher degree, complete a minimum of 250 hours of classroom training in three courses from a specified list that includes counseling and instructional skills training, and achieve an overall rating of excellent or higher on his/her last three instructor evaluations. Personnel awarded the Master Instructor Certificate are authorized to wear the AETC Master Instructor Badge. Those assigned to a survival school specialty code accumulate master points to qualify for the badge through training, experience, and education as specified in appropriate regulations.

Recruiting Badges

The U.S. Air Force has separate recruiting branches for the Air Force Reserve, the Air National Guard, and the active duty force. The badges worn by each element are shown in the color plates. The badges with the appropriate requirements for each are listed below.

USAF Recruiting Service Badges

The recruiting badges for the USAF active duty recruiting force are listed below with the requirements for each. The recruiting badges were redesigned in 1994 primarily to accommodate the redesignation of "United States Air Force Recruiting Service" as "Air Force Recruiting Service."

The BASIC USAF RECRUITING BADGE is awarded to all personnel assigned to an Air Force recruiting unit. Staff officers and support personnel wear the same basic badge as recruiters to designate assignment to USAF Recruiting Service. Recruiters are awarded this badge at completion of USAF Recruiting School at Lackland AFB, Texas. The basic badge has the Air Force Seal in the center and comes in two sizes: the small badge is 1 3/4 inch in diameter and the large badge is 2 1/2 inch in diameter. The new style basic badge without the words "United States" replaced the older style on January 1, 1995.

The SENIOR (SILVER) RECRUITING BADGE is awarded to all production recruiters who achieve 100 per cent in each of their assigned goaled programs over a 12 month period. They must achieve 115% in Net Reservation (Net Res) production or in Officer Training School/Health Professions (OTS/HP) production depending on their recruiting assignment. Flight supervisors may also be awarded this badge if they have been in their position for 12 months and the entire flight is 100% in all goaled programs, 115% in Net Res/HP production, and each recruiter in the flight is 100% in all goaled programs. In the Team Recruiting concept for HP, the team must be 100% in all goaled programs and 115% overall; if the team fails to meet the criteria no one on the team can receive the Senior Badge. The badge has a two inch diameter basic recruiting badge surrounded

by a silver wreath of oak leaves. The silver wreath on the badge was changed in 1994 from a dull pewter finish to a high gloss silver finish. The new style badges were first awarded at annual award banquets for fiscal 1994. Recruiters who had received the older style badge had them replaced with the high gloss version after January 1, 1995. Successive awards of this badge are denoted by a star on the top of the badge with a number that denotes the total cumulative number of times an individual has earned the senior badge. When the squadron's Rookie Recruiter of the year receives the senior badge, he will be awarded a badge with the letter "R" instead of a "1".

The MASTER (GOLD) RECRUITER BADGE is awarded annually to a unit's top recruiter. Governing criteria for this award is contained in applicable unit directives. This badge is awarded to the unit's top recruiter during the year. The badge design is identical to the Senior badge except that the wreath is gold in color with a gold star centered atop the badge.

Air National Guard (ANG) Recruiting Badges

Air National Guard Regulation 35-10 governs the wear of ANG recruiter badges. Assignment to Special Duty Identifier (SDI) 99500/0920 qualifies an individual to wear these badges.

The BASIC ANG RECRUITER BADGE is authorized for wear upon initial assignment as an Air National Guard recruiter. To qualify as a recruiter, the individual must have graduated from the ANG Recruiter Course at Lackland AFB, Texas. The badge is silver and measures 2 1/4 inches in diameter; it has the words "Air National Guard Recruiter" superimposed on the blue background of the badge.

The SENIOR LONGEVITY RECRUITER BADGE is authorized for wear upon completion of three years of ANG recruiting duty. The badge is the same as the basic badge except that it has a star above the badge.

The MASTER LONGEVITY RECRUITER BADGE is authorized for wear upon completion of six years of ANG recruiting duty. The badge is identical to the basic recruiter badge except it has a silver colored star encircled by a silver wreath atop the badge.

The ROOKIE RECRUITER of the YEAR BADGE is presented by the National Guard Bureau to the top ANG recruiter with less than two years of ANG recruiting duty. The badge is gold and may be worn until the recruiter is eligible for the Senior Recruiter Badge.

The RECRUITER of the YEAR BADGE (also known as the MASTER RECRUITER BADGE) is presented by the National Guard Bureau to the top ANG recruiter with more than two years of ANG recruiting duty. The badge is gold colored and has a gold star encircled by a gold wreath on the top center of the badge. The badge may be worn as long as the individual remains on recruiting duty.

Air Force Reserve Recruiting Badges

Air Force Reserve recruiting badges are governed by AFRES Pamphlet 10-105. Requirements for each badge are listed below.

The BASIC AIR FORCE RESERVE RECRUITING SERVICE BADGE may be worn by all Air Force Reserve Recruiting Service personnel who are not authorized to wear another recruiting badge. The badge is worn on all uniform combinations except the mess dress, BDUs, or adverse weather clothing. Male personnel wear the badge centered on the right breast pocket below the flap. Female personnel wear the badge centered with the lower edge 1/2 inch above the name tag.

The HEADQUARTERS AIR FORCE RESERVE RECRUITING STAFF BADGE is worn by headquarters recruiting staff personnel. The badge is the basic recruiting badge surrounded by a gold rope with the word "STAFF" in gold letters on a blue background at the bottom of the badge.

The SENIOR RECRUITER BADGE is worn by those Air Force Reserve personnel who are assigned as senior recruiters. The badge is the basic badge design with gold rope and the dark blue insert with the word "SENIOR" at the bottom of the badge.

A LINE SUPERVISOR BADGE is worn by Air Force Reserve personnel assigned to the E-8 position of wing line supervisor under the supervision of an E-9. The badge is the same as the Senior Recruiter Badge except the word "SENIOR" is on a light blue insert instead of the dark blue insert.

The MEDICAL RECRUITING BADGE is worn by Health Professions recruiters at both headquarters level and the basic unit level.

The CENTURY CLUB BADGES are authorized for wear by personnel who have attained 100 or more accession points during a fiscal year. "100" is for the first attainment of the century club, "200" for the second attainment and

"MASTER" for the third. Those Century Club recruiters who have attained positions as Staff, Senior, Line Supervisor, or Health Professions recruiters wear the DUAL CENTURY CLUB BADGE as long as they are assigned to those positions. As noted in the badge photos, the Century Club designations apply to the RECRUITING BADGE, the STAFF RECRUITING BADGE, the SENIOR RECRUITER BADGE, and the MEDICAL RECRUITING BADGE. It also applies to the LINE SUPERVISOR BADGE which is not shown since it is the same as the SENIOR RECRUITER BADGE except for the light blue insert that bears the word "Senior."

Fire Protection Badges

A FIRE PROTECTION BADGE is authorized for all fire protection personnel, military or civilian, assigned to a fire protection function. The proper level of the badge is determined by the individual's duty assignment. It is authorized for wear by personnel who have completed the fire protection apprentice school, currently at Goodfellow AFB, Texas and for many years previous at Chanute AFB, Illinois, and who are working in the fire protection career field.

FIREFIGHTER BADGE   *ASSISTANT FIRE CHIEF*   *DEPUTY FIRE CHIEF*   *FIRE CHIEF BADGE*

The FIREFIGHTER BADGE is awarded upon graduation from the Department of Defense Fire School and assignment as a fireman.

The FIRE CHIEF BADGE, the DEPUTY FIRE CHIEF BADGE, and the ASSISTANT FIRE CHIEF BADGE are awarded upon assignment to those positions. The Deputy Fire Chief acts as the First Sergeant for the Fire Chief.

Shooting Badges

Distinguished International Shooter Badge

Awarded by the National Board for the Promotion of Rifle Practice for outstanding performance in major international competition. It may be awarded to any US citizen who places first, second, third in rifle, pistol, or shotgun competition (individual or team). Also awarded to members of US international teams who place in the top 15 percent of all competitions in the Olympic Games, International Shooting Union, World Championship, Pan American Games, or the Championship of the Americas.

US Air Force Small Arms Marksmanship Badges

The following badges are awarded to Air Force personnel who attain an outstanding degree of unassisted achievement in certain recognized, individual competitions with the service pistol and rifle:

1. US Air Force Distinguished Rifleman Badge and Distinguished Pistol Shot Badge

Awarded to Air Force personnel in recognition for outstanding achievement in competitive target practice firing with the military service rifle; the award requires a specified number of points(30) attained from competition matches. Badge is gold, shield-shaped with a black and white target in the center; the shield is attached to a suspension bar that contains the words "U.S. Air Force."

Air Force personnel are recognized for outstanding achievement in competitive target practice firing with the military service pistol with the Distinguished Pistol Shot Badge ; the award requires a specified number of points (30) attained from competition matches. It is a gold, shield-shaped badge with a black and white target in the center and the words "U.S. Air Force" on the suspension bar.

2. Excellence-in-Competition (EIC) Badges

The Air Force awards these badges for excellence in individual competitions only. Awarded to any Air Force member who has earned the required number of credit points in recognized EIC rifle or pistol matches. Individuals may be awarded both badges, provided they earn the required number of points for each badge. All badges are awarded in silver and bronze. All badges are circular disks hanging from bars that contain the words "U.S. AIR FORCE."

A. The Silver EIC Rifle and Pistol Badges with Wreath

Award of this badge requires accumulation of 20 points in EIC rifle events.

B. The Bronze EIC Rifle and Pistol Badges with Wreath

Award of this badge requires accumulation of 6 points in EIC rifle events.

C. The Bronze EIC Rifle and Pistol Badges

Award of this badge requires accumulation of 4 points in EIC rifle events.

Special Duty Identification Badges

Vice Presidential Service Badge

Joint Chiefs of Staff Identification Badge

Presidential Service Badge

Office of the Secretary of Defense (OSD) Identification Badge

USAFA Permanent Professor Badge

Presidential Service Badge

The Presidential Service Badge was established on Sep 1, 1964. It replaced the White House Service Badge which had been established on Jun 1, 1960. The round badge bears a superimposed replica of the Presidential Coat of Arms. It is given by the President to Armed Forces personnel assigned to duty in the White House office or to military units and support facilities under the administration of the Military Assistant to the President for a period of at least one year, after January 20, 1961, as recognition, in a permanent way, of their contribution in the service of the President. Once earned, the badge becomes a permanent part of the recipient's uniform, and may be worn after the recipient leaves Presidential service.

Vice-Presidential Service Badge

The Vice-Presidential Service Badge was established on Jul 8, 1970. The seal of the Vice-President of the United States is superimposed on a white enameled disc surrounded by 27 gold rays radiating from the center. The badge is awarded in the name of the Vice-President to members of the armed forces who have been assigned to duty in the Office of the Vice-President for a period of at least one year after Jan 20, 1969. Once earned, the badge becomes a permanent part of the uniform.

Office of the Secretary of Defense (OSD) Identification Badge

This badge is worn by military personnel who are assigned on a permanent basis to the following organizational elements:

(1) Immediate offices of the Sec'y and Deputy Sec'y of Defense
(2) Offices of the Under Secretaries of Defense
(3) Offices of the Assistant Secretaries of Defense
(4) Office of the General Counsel of the Department of Defense
(5) Office of the Assistants to the Sec'y of Defense

(6) Office of the Defense Advisor, US Mission to the North Atlantic Treaty Organization (NATO)

After completion of one year of duty, the individual is entitled to permanent possession of the badge. A member of the Reserve Components who is assigned an authorized Reserve Forces position in OSD for a period of no less than two years, on or after Jan 1, 1973, is entitled to permanent possession of the badge.

Joint Chiefs of Staff Identification Badge

This badge is awarded to military personnel who have been assigned to duty and have served not less than 1 year after Jan 13, 1961 in a position of responsibility under the direct cognizance of the Joint Chiefs of Staff. The award of the badge must be approved by the Chairman, Joint Chiefs of Staff; the Director, Joint Staff; the head of a Directorate of the Joint Staff: or one of the subordinate agencies of the Organization of the Joint Chiefs of Staff. It consists of an oval silver metal wreath of laurel containing the shield of the United States superimposed on four gold metal unsheathed swords. The blades and grips of the swords are entwined with a gold metal scroll surrounding the shield with the words "JOINT CHIEFS OF STAFF" in blue enamel letters. Personnel are authorized to wear it following reassignment from duty with the JCS.

USAFA Permanent Professor Badge

The badge was approved by the USAF Chief of Staff on January 10, 1966. As of June 1995, regulations authorized 22 permanent professors at the U.S. Air Force Academy, including the Dean of the Faculty. A committee of three permanent professors screens and evaluates all prospective candidates and sends its list to the Academy Superintendent who makes the final selection. Permanent professors are appointed by the President, by and with the advice and consent of the Senate.

USAF Academy Badges

Commandant's Pin

Cadets' names must appear on the Commandant's list for obtaining a Military Performance Average of 3.0 or above for the previous semester to wear this badge. Fourth class cadets must have a 3.0 or better average during Basic Cadet Training to be eligible for this badge.

Superintendent's Pin

To wear this badge, cadets' names must appear on the Superintendent's list for having a Grade Point Average, Military Performance Average, and a Physical Education Average of 3.0. This pin is awarded to a cadet whose name appears on the Commandant's list, the Dean's list, and the Athletic list.

Dean's Pin

Cadets' names must appear on the Dean's list for obtaining a Grade Point Average of 3.0 or better for the previous semester to be eligible for this badge.

Commandant's/Dean's Pin

Awarded to cadets whose names appear on both the Commandant's list and the Dean's list.

Athletic Pin

To be eligible for this badge, cadets must meet the following criteria: 3.0 Physical Education Average (PEA) or higher. The PEA is based on 50% Physical Education, class grades from previous semester, 40% PFT, and 10% AFT.

Dean's/Athletic Pin

Awarded to those cadets whose names appear on both the Dean's and Athletic lists.

Commandant's/Athletic Pin

Awarded to those cadets whose names appear on both the Commandant's and Athletic lists.

USAFA Cadet Hat Badges

Worn on the cadet's dress hat. The eagle is the same as an USAF officer cap device without the star filled circle above the eagle's head. Gold Prop Insignia is worn on the cadet flight cap and indicates a relative served in the AAF. The silver is the standard flight cap insignia after recognization at the end of the freshman year.

Cadet Flight Wings

Cadets who have soloed a USAF Academy glider, T-3, or USAFA Aero Club Aircraft while enrolled in an Airmanship course are entitled to wear these wings. Center of the badge has the Federal shield emblem that is on the USAF pilot badge.

Cadet Instructor Pilot Wings

Cadets who have soloed a USAF Academy glider, T-3, or USAFA Aero Club Aircraft while enrolled in an Airmanship course and have completed instructor upgrade training are entitled to wear these wings with a star. Cadet instructor pilots provide most ground and flight instructions.

Cadet Senior Instructor Pilot Wings

Aviation cadets who complete upgrade training and have at least 100 hours on instructor sorties are entitled to wear the Cadet Senior Instructor Pilot Wings.

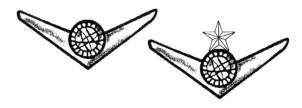

Cadet Navigator Instructor Wings

These wings are worn by cadet navigator instructors. A star is added for a senior cadet aviation instructor, a rating obtained after satisfying minimum sortie/hour requirements. Center of the badge is an armillary sphere which is also on the World War II Army Air Force navigator wings.

Parachutist Badge

To wear this badge, cadets must complete the Army Airborne School, Fort Benning, Georgia, or the Airmanship Parachuting Course taught by the Parachuting Branch of the USAF Academy. The badge is the same as that worn by USAF personnel and may be transferred to the officer uniform upon commissioning. Senior and Master badges are awarded in accordance with USAF regulations .

Recondo Badge

This badge is awarded to cadets who have completed the Department of the Army's course in small unit combat leadership instruction conducted by the Fourth Infantry Division (Mech), Fort Carson, Colorado.

Air Assault Badge

Cadets who have completed air assault school are authorized to wear this badge. This is the same badge authorized for wear by U.S. Army and USAF personnel and may be transferred to the officer uniform when the cadet is commissioned.

Bulldog Badge

This badge is authorized for cadets who have completed the Marine Corps Bulldog program at Quantico, Virginia. The brass badge is identical to the U.S. Marine Corps enlisted collar insignia.

Patches of the Army Air Force and the U.S. Air Force

The patches displayed on page 71 are representative of the types of patches used in both the Army Air Force and the United States Air Force from 1941 to present day. There are many other styles and designs that cannot be included here because of space limitations. A complete work on Air Force patches would be a monumental task and impressive achievement. My intent here is simply to provide some examples of the style and use of Air Force patches.

My experiences in helping veterans to create displays to honor their military service has shown me that the single most important item to a veteran other than perhaps a significant decoration would be a unit patch. Unfortunately, many veterans do not keep their original unit patches and are disappointed when they find out later that it is unlikely that they will ever find one. While patches can be made from original patch designs, it is usually cost prohibitive to have just one or several made. If I could convince any veteran of one thing, it would be to keep the uniform insignia that they wore during their service because to lose it is to lose a part of their identity. While it seemed unimportant at the time, I did keep at least one of each of my unit patches throughout my Air Force career and now I treasure those items more than I ever could have when wearing them. The patch has always been an important part of the Air Force uniform -- it has always stirred the emotions of loyalty, comradeship, and pride as well as identity with the mission and organization. With a few exceptions such as the 11th and 12th Air Forces, the Army Air Force numbered air force patches were circular in design with a blue background. Cloth patches of the period were mostly "unmerrowed", that is, they were unstitched around the edges. As methods improved, the patch edges were sewn to prevent unraveling; this stitch method was perfected in the 1950s by The Merrow Sewing Machine Company who produced a machine that would make a heavy overlock stitch around the outer perimeter of a patch, hence the term "merrowed" which would become a characteristic of patches from that point on. Patches have been made from different cloth materials, including cotton, wool, linen, and leather. some of the finest and most sought after patches are the flying squadron patches worn on the flight jackets of Army Air Force personnel during World War II; they are often beautifully colored and designed and about 5-6 inches in diameter. They are valued items to both collectors and veterans of the period.

The Army Air Force patches shown on the first line are typical of those worn during World War II. Many of the numbered air force patches of that period are available today since there are still many requests for them by veterans who wish to display their memorabilia of the period. The last patch on the first line is the aviation cadet patch worn by cadets in the AAF flying training program during World War II. This patch, with golden orange wing and propeller device was worn on the right sleeve, was primarily seen with a blue background although a patch of the same design but with a black background was also worn during that same period.

Army Air Force Regulation 35-12 on March 1, 1943 created five categories of enlisted technical specialists and authorized the wearing of an ultramarine blue triangular patch to designate one of the five assigned occupational fields. The 2 1/2 inch equilateral triangle patches, which are shown on the second line, with the gold colored specialty emblems were worn centered on the outside of the right sleeve four inches above the lower edge of the sleeve of the coat, field jacket, and shirt; it was also worn on the left breast pocket of the fatigue uniform.

The five specified occupational fields were:

1. **Armament Specialist** which was denoted by a falling bomb. It was worn by nine occupations which included Aerial Torpedo Mechanic, Antiaircraft Machine Gunner, and Bombsight Mechanic.

2. **Communications Specialist** which depicts a tower between four flashes. It was worn by 22 different occupational fields that included radio Operator, Control Tower Operator, Communication chief, Cryptographer, radio Mechanics, Radio Observers, Telephone & Telegraph Lineman, and Wire Chief.

3. **Engineering Specialist** which shows the silhouette of an engine. It was worn by 33 different occupational fields including Airplane Inspector, crew chief, Line Chief, Flight chief, mechanical specialist, Depot Engineer Chief, Parachute Shop Chief, Parachute Rigger and Repairman, Glider Mechanic, and Welder.

4. **Photography Specialist** which depicts a camera. It was worn by nine occupational specialties including Camera Technician, Photographic Chief, Photographic Interpreter, Photographic Laboratory Chief, and Motion Picture Cameraman.

5. **Weather Specialist** which depicts a weather vane. It was worn by six occupations including Weather Cryptographer, Forecaster, Observer, Station Chief, and Radio Sonde Operator.

The meritorious unit commendation, or "toilet seat" patch as it is often referred to, was awarded to units of the AAF during WWII for exceptionally meritorious conduct on or after Jan. 1, 1944. Successive awards were denoted by the addition of numerals in the center of the wreath; some versions of the patch had a star in the center of the wreath. The patch was worn on the lower portion of the right sleeve. The horizontal stripe is the overseas service bar which was worn on the lower left portion of the AAF service coat; each stripe denoted six months service overseas in a combat theater. The slanted service stripe was worn on the left sleeve at a 45 degree angle just above any overseas bars worn; each service stripe represented at least three years continuous active service. The honorable service patch or "ruptured duck" (same design as the honorable service pin) was worn above the right pocket of the AAF service coat at the time of discharge to indicate honorable service during WWII.

The Strategic Air Command (SAC) and Tactical Air Command (TAC) patches are representative of the command level patches worn during most of the Air Force's short history. The shield design used for those patches carried over to the newer command patches created in the last several years; examples shown are the newly created Air Combat Command (ACC) and Air Education & Training Command (AETC) patches. Representative examples of squadron, wing, and group patches are shown on the next line.

The last two lines show examples of training unit patches, novelty patches, and specialty patches along with an Aerospace Defense command and a 96th Bomb Wing patch. Training class patches for a navigator training class and a pilot training class are shown; patches like these are some of the hardest to find since they were made in small quantities usually to accommodate class sizes of 50 to 100 personnel. Navigator class 70-16's patch shows a T-29 aircraft, for many years the primary training aircraft, flying under the Golden Gate Bridge, which was a familiar landmark when the USAF Navigator Training School was located at Mather AFB near Sacramento, CA. A pilot training class 70-01 patch from Moody AFB, Georgia is also shown with a Latin inscription around the edges which is professed to mean "Don't let the bastards get you down!"

Patches of the Army Air Force

Many of the patches worn by Army Air Force personnel are depicted on page 52,53, courtesy of J.L. Pete Morgan and Ted A. Thurman, authors of the <u>American Military Patch Guide</u> which shows these patches in actual color as they were worn during World War II. These patches are shown as an aid to help Army Air Force veterans and their families to identify the patches of the units with which the veteran served. Squadron and group patches are not shown simply because of the numbers of patches and frankly because of the availability of those patches -- most are rare and, if they can be found as originals, would be very costly. An alternative for the veteran and his/her family who are looking for that particular squadron or group patch is to contact the Office of Air Force History to obtain the design of the patch and perhaps have it recreated. The reproduction of patches could be expensive if done in small quantities.

The numbered Air Forces patches are led by the Army Air Force patch. The First, Second, Third, and Fourth Air Forces were based in the continental U.S.; the Sixth was in the Caribbean; Fifth, Seventh, Thirteenth, and Twentieth were in the Pacific; the Eleventh was in Alaska; the Fourteenth (the Flying Tigers) was in China; the Tenth was in India; and the Eighth, Ninth, Twelfth, and Fifteenth Air Forces were in the European Theater. The Eighteenth Air Force was created in 1951 and based in the U.S.

Major Air Command (MAJCOM) patches follow the numbered Air Force patches. Most of these patches are very difficult to obtain. The first patch of this group belonged to the U.S. Strategic Air Force which consisted of the Eighth and Fifteenth Air Forces in the European Theater. The U.S. Army Airways Communication System, the Air Transport Command, the Airborne Troop Carrier Command, and the Far East Air Force are some of the most sought after patches from the AAF period.

The remaining specialized patches shown include some rare varieties such as the WASP, the AAF Flight Instructor, and the AAF Cadet patches. The triangular AAF Technician Specialists patches are shown also; these patches are shown on the color plates and are explained in detail elsewhere in the book. The last patches shown are the "arc" tabs which were authorized in 1945 and were worn directly over the Army Air Force shoulder insignia.

All of these patches have a significant individual history and, collectively, tell the story of the Army Air Force. Hopefully, the inclusion of these patches will stir an interest in the veteran and collector to continue research into the background of these units and learn more about their contributions to our success in World War II. Excellent sources are available to gather this material from specific authors or the Office of Air Force History and the Air Force Historical Research Agency.

☑ U.S. ARMY AIR FORCE

☑ 1st AIR FORCE

☑ 2nd AIR FORCE

☑ 3rd AIR FORCE

☑ 4th AIR FORCE

☑ 5th AIR FORCE

☑ 6th AIR FORCE

☑ 7th AIR FORCE

☑ 8th AIR FORCE

☑ 9th AIR FORCE

☑ 10th AIR FORCE

☑ 11th AIR FORCE

☑ 12th AIR FORCE

☑ 13th AIR FORCE

☑ 14th AIR FORCE

☐ 15th AIR FORCE

☐ 18th AIR FORCE

☑ 20th AIR FORCE

☑ U.S. STRATEGIC AIR FORCE

☑ U.S. ARMY AIRWAYS COMMUNICATION SYS.

☑ DESERT AIR FORCE

☐ TROOP CARRIER COMMAND

☑ U.S. AIR FORCE EUROPE

☑ CUBAN AIR FORCE

☐ WOMEN'S AIR FERRYING CMD.

☑ MILITARY AIR TRANSPORT SERVICE

☑ ALASKAN AIR COMMAND

☐ CONTINENTAL AIR COMMAND

☑ ALLIED AIR FORCE MEDITERRANEAN

☑ AIR UNIVERSITY

☑ AIR MATERIAL COMMAND

☑ U.S. ARMY AIR FORCE HEADQUARTERS CMD.

☑ AIR TRANS. COMMAND

☑ A/B TROOP CARRIER
☑ AIR FERRYING COMMAND
☑ AIR TRANS. CMD. GROUND PERS.
☑ AIR TRAINING COMMAND
☑ AIR FORCE R.O.T.C.
☐ 9th ENGR. COMMAND

☐ 12th TACTICAL AIR FORCE
☐ PHILIPPINE AIR FORCE
☑ FAR EAST AIR FORCE
☑ AIR TECHNICAL SERVICE CMD., EUROPE
☐ COMBAT AIR CREW

☑ U.S. TECHNICAL REPRESENTATIVE
☑ AIR FORCE CADET
☐ U.S. AIR FORCE INSTRUCTOR
☐ U.S. AIR CORPS (OLD)
☐ ARMY AIR FORCE FLIGHT GUNNERY SCHOOL

☐ WOMEN'S ARMY SERVICE PILOT
☐ PHILIPPINE AIR FORCE
☐ ARMY AF, HQ, VARIATION
☐ THUNDERBIRD FIELD, ARIZONA
☑ U.S. AAF FLIGHT INSTRUCTOR
☐ AIR DEFENSE COMMAND

☑ AIR FORCE ENGINEERING SPECIALIST
☑ AIR FORCE PHOTOGRAPHY SPECIALIST
☑ AIR FORCE WEATHER SPECIALIST
☑ AIR FORCE ARMAMENT SPECIALIST
☑ AIR FORCE COMMUNICATION SPECIALIST
☑ ALASKAN AIR DEPOT

AAF ARCS

☐ A.A.F. SCHOOL
☑ TACTICAL AIR COMMAND
☑ PERSONNEL DISTRIBUTION COMMAND
☐ MOBILE DISPLAY UNIT

☑ A.A.F.S.
☑ AIR TRANSPORT COMMAND
☑ I TROOP CARRIER COMMAND
☑ TACTICAL CENTER

53

Enlisted Rank Insignia

The rank insignia for the USAF has maintained its same basic design since it was authorized after the USAF became a separate service on September 18, 1947. Previous to this date, in the AAF, the Air Force rank insignia was the same as that of the Army ground forces.

The "Army style" rank is shown on the following pages in order of lowest rank to highest. Those ranks that include a "T" are technician specialist ranks that were created to allow for promotion with appropriate pay increases without granting Non-Commissioned Officer (NCO) status. USAF enlisted personnel continued to wear the "Army " rank even after the newly authorized USAF rank was approved in 1948.

Sergeant   Technician 4th grade

An examination of many photographs throughout the USAF's early period revealed that many USAF enlisted personnel continued to wear "Army" rank as well as Army uniforms during the Korean War era even while many others wore the blue uniform with USAF style rank insignia. Although the Air Force blue uniform was adopted on January 25, 1949, it was not available for issue until 1952 although USAF rank was available earlier. Some members actually wore USAF rank on Army uniforms.

Technician 3rd grade   Staff Sergeant

As related to me by an Air Force veteran of the period, if an individual was promoted while still wearing the Army uniform, he was required to wear the Air Force rank insignia on the Army uniform even if the combination looked strange! Although an exact date is hard to obtain and may not exist, it appears that the transition from Army rank to USAF rank was essentially completed sometime after the Korean War.

In 1948, General Hoyt S. Vandenberg approved the design of the U.S. Air Force enlisted rank that would maintain its same basic design to present day. The only documentation available that indicates approval for the chevron design that remains today are the minutes from a March 9, 1948, Pentagon meeting which states that chevron designs were circulated at Bolling AFB, Washington D.C. At that time a group of 150 soldiers were polled and the majority selected the design in use today. The star on the chevron is most likely taken from the star design that was incorporated with military aircraft markings that were used as early as 1916. While the design of the rank has remained basically the same, distinct changes have occurred during its evolution to the present day design.

There were four major changes to the enlisted rank structure that stand out in its development: (1) the addition of senior NCO ranks (Senior Master Sergeant and Chief Master Sergeant); (2) the replacement of the white star by the blue star to reflect non-NCO ranks; (3) the eventual elimination of the "blue star" ranks; and (4) the change in the number of upper stripes for the senior NCO grades (E-7 thru E-9). The initial enlisted rank structure approved in 1948 is shown in the table. While the stripe design was different from the Army rank, the titles given to those stripes still reflected Army influence. Note that there was no "first sergeant" rank designation; Master Sergeant was the only grade approved for first sergeant duties at that time. Chevrons were four inches in width for men and three inches in width for women. When the 1505 (khaki) uniform was authorized in 1961, the three inch chevron had to be used for men as well as women on that uniform.

Technical Sergeant

On February 20, 1950, General Vandenberg directed the change of nomenclature for USAF enlisted personnel from "Soldiers" to "Airmen." This change led to the renaming of the titles for the chevron style rank in 1952. The lower three grades now reflected the "Airman" title instead of the previous Army titles. Grades above the airmen ranks still reflected the previous titles. There was now a clear distinction in titles and chevron design between the "Airmen" grades and the NCO (Sergeant) grades. To provide distinction and recognition to those Master Sergeants serving as First Sergeants, General Nathan Twining approved the First Sergeant's insignia on September 22, 1954. The diamond (or lozenge) insignia became available on September 21, 1955.

Master Sergeant   1st Sgt

After The Military Pay Act of 1958 created the additional grades of E-8 and E-9, new insignia was designed and approved for the two top enlisted grades. The E-8 grade, Senior Master Sergeant, was created on September 1, 1958 and the E-9 grade, Chief Master Sergeant was created on December 1, 1959. One inverted chevron was added to the Master Sergeant chevrons to signify the new Senior Master Sergeant rank and two inverted chevrons were added to signify the new Chief Master Sergeant rank. In 1959 the title of Basic Airman for grade E-1(no rank insignia) was changed to Airman Basic. The table also shows the First Sergeant lozenge with all three of the senior NCO grades.

On March 3, 1967, distinctive insignia for the Chief Master Sergeant of the Air Force was approved. In lieu of adding a third stripe atop the Chief Master Sergeant chevron, a wreath was added to encircle the star in the middle of

Chief Master
Sergeant

Chief Master Sergeant of the
Air Force

the chevron. It's ironic that a third stripe on top was eliminated primarily because of the "super zebra" effect of too many stripes but in later years a third stripe would be added to all senior NCO ranks! Granted, one stripe was removed from the bottom but the effect, in my view, was the same.

On October 19, 1967, major changes were made in the titles of grades E-1 to E-4. The most significant change was the restoration of NCO status to the E-4 grade whose title had been changed from Sergeant to Airman First Class in 1952. Giving NCO status to the E-4 grade not only aligned the Air Force E-4 grade with the other services but also gave the E-4 grade added prestige and privileges which improved Air Force retention rates. The titles "Airman Second Class" and "Airman Third Class" were replaced with "Airman" and "Airman First Class," respectively. The new titles are reflected in the table.

Several different proposals to completely revamp the enlisted rank structure and titles were made in the mid-1970's but were never acted upon. On December 30, 1975, it was announced that new insignia would be implemented that would clearly distinguish the Airmen and NCO grades. The major change required that the stripes for the Airmen grades have a blue star instead of a white (or silver) star which would only be on the NCO chevrons. (The star was considered as

Senior
Airman, E4

Sergeant E4

removed although it became a blue star on the cloth chevrons and no star on the metal chevron.) This change also mandated the two titles for the E-4 grade, Senior Airman which would have three stripes and a blue star and Sergeant which would have three stripes with white star as well as accompanying NCO status. In my associations with Air Force veterans, I've seen this era of rank insignia to be the most difficult to recall and understand; the difficulty in understanding may have been in some measure one of the reasons for its demise later. The new rank structure was implemented on June 1, 1976 and is reflected in that column in the table on page 56. This rank structure would remain in place until 1991.

In an effort to improve the declining ratio of Airmen to NCOs, Air Force Chief of Staff, General Merril McPeak, on March 19, 1991 announced the termination of the E-4 NCO, effective May 2, 1991. In October of that year, new enlisted insignia was proposed and mandated for wear in October 1999 (the implementation date was later changed to October 1, 1997). The blue star was removed from all Airmen rank chevrons and was replaced with the white star

of the NCO chevrons. The stripes and star of the new rank insignia were much brighter than the silver-tinted insignia that had been in use for the past 43 years. Both the stripes and star on the enlisted chevron are bright white.

Other than the elimination of the E-4 Sergeant rank, the most significant change of this period was the addition of one stripe atop each of the senior NCO chevrons (E-7, E-8, E-9). Master Sergeant now had a single chevron on top while Senior Master Sergeant had two atop and Chief Master Sergeant had three.

Chief Master Sergeant
1st Sgt. (old)

Chief Master Sergeant
1st Sgt. (new)

The change in rank insignia for the first time clearly distinguished the top three Senior NCO ranks from other NCOs. Until the E-4 Sergeants were either promoted or separated, the Air Force would have both Sergeants and Senior Airmen wearing the same style rank, three chevrons and accompanying white star, although Sergeants were wearing the older style insignia which was more silver-tinted and less bright than the new style insignia. The table shows the enlisted rank structure as it is today.

Perhaps the USAF has finally latched onto a rank structure that will become permanent and ultimately a tradition. While most of the changes can be attributed to the Air Force's development as a new service and its search for tradition, some of the changes seem unnecessary and probably could have been avoided. While some may say that the changes reflect progress, I believe that some of those that occurred during my service were both confusing and unnecessary. The confusion factor can easily be born out by asking USAF personnel to correctly identify the enlisted rank structure during varying periods of the Air Force's history. It becomes even more confusing when members of the other branches of the military try to figure it out. The present rank structure makes sense, looks good, and is easily understandable - good reasons for keeping it that way for today's and tomorrow's Air Force!

Chief Master Sergeant of the
Air Force

United States Air Force Enlisted Ranks 1947 to Present

	E 1	E 2	E 3	E 4	E 5	E 6
1947	Seventh grade Private (no insignia)	Sixth grade Private First Class	Fifth grade Corporal / Technician 5th grade	Fourth grade Sergeant / Technician 4th grade	Third grade Staff Sergeant / Technician 3rd grade	Second grade Technical Sergeant
1948	Private (no insignia)	Private First Class	Corporal	Sergeant	Staff Sergeant	Technical Sergeant
1952	Basic Airman (no insignia)	Airman 3rd Class	Airman 2rd Class	Airman 1st Class	Staff Sergeant	Technical Sergeant
1959	Airman Basic no Insignia	Airman 3rd Class	Airman 2nd class	Airman 1st class	Staff Sergeant	Technical Sergeant
1967	Airman Basic (no insignia)	Airman 3rd Class	Airman 2nd Class	Airman 1st Class	Staff Sergeant	Technical Sergeant
1976	Airman Basic (no insignia)	Airman	Airman 1st Class	Senior Airman, E4 / Sergeant E4	Staff Sergeant	Technical Sergeant
1991	Airman Basic (no insignia)	Airman	Airman 1st Class	Senior Airman	Staff Sergeant	Technical Sergeant

United States Air Force Enlisted Ranks 1947 to Present

Highlights of Enlisted rank changes

1947 - USAAF becomes USAF
1948 - USAF design approved
1950 - Enlisted personnel referred to as "Airmen" vs. "Soldiers"
1952 - Titles changed from Army descriptions to new USAF
1954 - First Sergeant Insignia approved
1958 - New grades, E-8 and E-9, authorized
1967 - CMSgt of AF Insignia approved
1967 - NCO status restored to E-4
1976 - New design rank approved for E-1 through E-4
1991 - Sgt (E-4) rank terminated, current design approved

Year	E 7	E 8	E 9	E 9
1947	First grade — Master Sergeant / First Sergeant			
1948	Master Sergeant			
1952	Master Sergeant			
1959	Master Sergeant / 1st Sgt	Senior Master Sergeant / 1st Sgt.	Chief Master Sergeant / 1st Sgt.	
1967	Master Sergeant / 1st Sgt	Senior Master Sergeant / 1st Sgt.	Chief Master Sergeant / 1st Sgt	Chief Master Sergeant of the Air Force
1976	Master Sergeant / 1st Sgt	Senior Master Sergeant / 1st Sgt.	Chief Master Sergeant / 1st Sgt.	Chief Master Sergeant of the Air Force
1991	Master Sergeant / 1st Sgt.	Senior Master Sergeant / 1st Sgt.	Chief Master Sergeant / 1st Sgt.	Chief Master Sergeant of the Air Force

Officer Rank Insignia

Rank insignia was first authorized during the Revolutionary War to distinguish offices and their different levels of responsibility or grade. Initially, colored cockades were placed on hats and then General and Special Staff officers wore a wide specifically colored ribbon across their chest to identify their level of command or responsibility.

The shoulder insignia we use today evolved from about 1780 when Brigadier General were designated with one star on each epaulet, Major Generals 2 stars and by 1799 three stars for the rank of Lt. General.

Embroidered shoulder straps began replacing epaulets for field duty about 1836-37 and specific insignia for each grade was designated. The most junior officer rank, the lieutenant, was created in the British Navy in the 16th century to provide an officer ready and able to take command should the "captain" be absent or unable to command. Taken from French words meaning "to take the place of", the lieutenant's duty was often to be his superior officer's deputy.

First Lieutenants were identified with one gold bar, Captains with 2 gold bars, Majors used gold embroidered leaves. Earlier (about 1832) gold eagles had been designated for Infantry Colonels and silver eagles for Colonels of all other branches. Later when it was decided all Colonels would wear the same color eagles, it was more practical to switch to the predominant color silver, additionally influenced by the fact that General officer's stars were silver.

The original 1832 order which created the rank of Lieutenant Colonel specified silver as were most of the Colonel insignia then.

So through the Civil War, Captain's and Lieutenant's bars were gold. Both grades were changed to silver after the Civil War and when the rank of 2nd Lieutenant was created in WWI the single bar was made gold while 1st Lieutenant remained silver.

The Army officer rank of World War II was carried over from the Army Air Force to the U.S. Air Force uniform where it has remained essentially unchanged except for a brief period in 1994 when the Air Force officer service coat was redesigned with sleeve rank, consisting of 1/4 and 1/2 inch stripes place two inches above the end of the sleeve. Large style rank insignia has been worn on the flight cap as well as the service coat and rain coat. Smaller rank insignia was worn on the lapels and on the light blue short sleeve shirt until epaulet rank insignia was designed. The insignia design and color on the officer epaulet rank remained the same as the metal rank it replaced. The epaulet rank was well received because of the ease with which it was attached to the uniform; it eliminated the need for measuring or "eyeballing" the correct placement of the metal insignia on the short sleeve shirt.

The current men and women's service coat still use the metal pin-on rank. Subdued officer grade insignia was designed for wear on the battle dress uniform; it was both pinned and sewn on. Except for the darkened "subdued" color, it is of the same design as that used for other uniforms.

The officer rank insignia of the Air Force is probably the most traditional aspect of the uniform since its design remains the same. Although consideration was given to changing the officer rank design when the U.S. Air Force became a separate service in 1947, the idea was scrapped in favor of keeping the rank style used by the U.S. Army and the U.S. Army Air Force. By doing so, the United States Air Force will always be able to trace it roots through its officer rank insignia which to this day has endured and will always provide a clear link to its past and future.

Warrant Officer and Flight Officers

The warrant officer rank was created to fill special positions requiring greater technical skill and responsibility than an NCO but without the responsibility of command. The military grade of warrant officer originated several hundred years ago during the early period of the British Navy. The less experienced officers of the Royal Navy relied heavily on the technical expertise, knowledge, and allegiance of senior sailors who were rewarded with a Royal Warrant. The Royal Warrant designation clearly distinguished them from the other sailors while maintaining the strict class system of the period.

The rank and grade of warrant officer was established on July 7, 1918. Until 1942 when their role was expanded, warrant officers performed functions such as mine planting, band leading, administration, and supply. In 1941, Congress authorized two grades, chief warrant officer and warrant officer junior grade, and also authorized flight pay for those performing aerial flight duties. It was defined in 1942 as a rank above all enlisted ranks and immediately below all commissioned officers. On January 11, 1942, gold and red bars were approved as warrant officer insignia, and in September, 1942, an ultramarine blue and golden-orange bar was approved for the newly adopted warrant grade of flight officer. In May of 1945, a peak of almost 57,000 warrant officers were on active duty in both the U.S. Army and U.S. Army Air Force.

Army Air Force

Flight Officer - A gold colored bar, one inch long and 3/8 inch wide, with rounded ends and a blue enamel top. It has a 1/8 inch latitudinal gold stripe across the center.

Warrant Officer Junior Grade - A gold colored bar, one inch long and 3/8 inch wide, with rounded ends and a red enamel top. It has a 1/8 inch latitudinal gold stripe across the center.

Chief Warrant Officer - A gold colored bar, one inch long and 3/8 inch wide, with rounded ends and a red enamel top. It has a 1 inch longitudinal gold stripe running the length of the bar.

United States Air Force

Warrant Officer, WO1 - One gold-colored bar of the same type as for a CWO-2, with two blue enamel blocks arranged in the same manner as for a CWO-3. All USAF Warrant Officer insignia was 1 1/8" by 3/8". Miniature insignia was 3/4" long.

Chief Warrant Officer, CWO2 - One gold-colored bar of the same type as for a second lieutenant, with three blue enamel blocks arranged in the same manner as for a CWO-4.

Chief Warrant Officer, CWO3 - One silver-colored bar of the same type as for a CWO-4, with two blue enamel blocks superimposed. Shoulder insignia blocks are 3/8 inch wide and 1/4 inch apart. Collar insignia; blocks are 1/4 inch wide and 5/32 inch apart.

Chief Warrant Officer, CWO4 - One silver-colored bar of the same type as for a first lieutenant, with three blue enamel blocks superimposed. Shoulder insignia; center enamel block is 1/4 inch wide, with 1/8 inch wide outer blocks, 1/4 inch from the edges of the center block. Collar insignia; center enamel block is 5/32 inch wide, with 3/32 inch wide outer blocks, 5/32 inch from the edges of the center block.

U.S. Air Force Commissioned Rank Insignia

With the exception of the warrant officer and flight officer grades, the Army Air Force officer rank is the same design as that used today by the United States Air Force. Only for a brief period from 1993 to 1994 the USAF had officer rank insignia that was radically different from both the previous and current design; this rank was often referred to as "airline pilot rank" or "navy style rank." The initial popularity of this insignia is debatable but there was quite an outpour of dissension with the new insignia that to many (author included) was both unnecessary and too different from the past insignia, thereby destroying a tradition of rank in the interest of "simplifying" the uniform. Eventually the new insignia was scrapped in favor of the older, more accepted insignia.

While officer rank has been worn in many different ways, i.e. metal, cloth, embroidered, epaulet-style, and miniature, it is depicted here primarily in the regular-size metal style which clearly shows the proper design of the rank. The "airline pilot" style rank which was short-lived is depicted.

metal style   epaulet-style   "airline pilot" style rank

 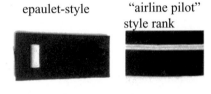

Second Lieutenant - One gold-colored bar of the same type as for a first lieutenant. Typically, the entry level commissioned officer rank; an exception being the medical career fields which may offer higher entry ranks depending on training and experience levels. While some second lieutenants may immediately assume their duty responsibilities upon commissioning, most spend a majority of their second lieutenant time in a training status, preparing for their first assignment in their specialty. Bar rank measures 1" by 3/8" for regular size and 3/4" long for miniature.

First Lieutenant - One silver-colored bar of the same type as for a captain. Increased responsibility assignments as staff officers, branch chiefs, and primary aircrew members are typical of this rank. In the 17th century, the lieutenant rank in Great Britain was given to those noblemen in training to become captains. Bar rank is 1" by 3/8" for regular size and 3/4" long for miniature.

Captain - Two smooth silver-colored bars, without bevel, attached at each end by a holding bar. Shoulder insignia; each bar slightly curved, 1-1/8 inches long by 3/8 inch wide, and 3/8 inch apart. Collar insignia; flat, each bar 3/4 inch long by 1/4 inch wide and 1/4 inch apart. Assignments for this rank may include flight commanders, branch chiefs, staff officers, and squadron commanders.

Major - A seven-pointed, silver-colored oak leaf, raised and veined. Shoulder insignia; slightly curved, one inch from stem tip to center leaf tip. Collar insignia; flat, 23/32 inch from stem tip to center leaf tip. The term was taken from the Latin word meaning "greater." The rank initially evolved from the rank of sergeant major, which in the 16th century was just below lieutenant colonel. In succeeding centuries, the rank became "major" as the "sergeant" portion was dropped. Bar rank is 1 1/8" from top to end of stem for regular size and 3/4" for miniature.

Lieutenant Colonel - A seven-pointed, silver-colored oak leaf, raised and veined. Shoulder insignia; slightly curved, one inch from stem tip to center leaf tip. Collar insignia; flat, 23/32 inch from stem tip to center leaf tip. Bar rank is 1 1/8" for regular size and 3/4" for miniature.

Colonel - A silver-colored spread eagle, made in pairs, right and left, talons of one foot grasping an olive branch, the other, a bundle of arrows. Shoulder insignia; slightly curved, with 1-1/2-inch wing span. Collar insignia; flat, with 31/32-inch wing span. The term evolved in the 16th century from the Spanish king, Ferdinand, who called the commander of his columns "cabo de colunela" which later became colonel in the French and British armies. The current pronunciation of "kernel" was established by the British.

Brigadier General - One silver-colored star, 1" in height for regular size and 3/8" for collar size. Officer sleeve rank a 2" embroidered strip worn 2 inches from the end of the sleeve.

Major General - Two silver-colored stars of the same type and arranged in the same manner as for a lieutenant general. Sleeve rank - one 1/2" stripe above 2" embroidered stripe.

Lieutenant General - Three silver-colored stars, of the same type and arranged in the same manner as for a general, except the distance between centers of adjacent shoulder stars is one inch. Sleeve rank - two 1/2" stripes above a 2" embroidered stripe.

General - Four silver-colored, five-pointed, pyramid-shaped stars. Shoulder stars are one inch in diameter and are either fastened together on a metal holding bar or placed individually with one point of each star in the same line; distance between the centers of adjacent stars is 3/4 inch. Collar stars are 9/16 inch in diameter and are fastened together on a metal holding bar in a straight line with one ray of each star pointing upward and at right angles to the holding bar. General Daniel "Chappie" James became the first black officer to achieve four star rank in the U.S. military on September 1, 1975. On October 1, 1989, General Hansford T. Johnson became the first USAF Academy graduate to attain four star rank. Sleeve rank - three 1/2" stripes above a 2" embroidered stripe.

General of the Air Force - Five silver stars at each of five points, joined together in a pentagonal pattern. General Henry "Hap" Arnold was the first airman to hold five star rank when he became General of the Army on December 21, 1944.

Introduction to the Color Plates

The military medal color plates are organized to follow the Air Force order of precedence for decorations, service medals, ribbons, and unit awards. Army decorations used for the Army Air Force veterans during World War II and for U.S. Air Force veterans are included just behind the equivalent USAF decorations. The plates start at the top with the Medal of Honor and progress down to the foreign service medals authorized to Air Force personnel for service in a particular campaign.

Each color medal or ribbon is referenced to a more detailed description in the text section of the book. The final color plate shows a current Air Force ribbon chest in the correct order of precedence from World War II to the present. (Army Air Force veterans should note that unit citations are included here per current regulations although prior to 1947 unit citations were worn separately). The facing page to the color ribbon page shows the attachments that are authorized for each ribbon and the adjacent legend details their use.

After the medal color plates there is a page devoted to patches of the Air Force. A sampling of representative patches from the Army Air Force period to the present day U.S. Air Force style are shown. Patches are labeled and are explained in the associated text write-up.

The next color plate features layouts of veterans' awards displays for World War II, Korea, Vietnam, Southwest Asia (Persian Gulf), and peacetime service. The purpose of this page is to show examples of how veterans might combine their awards and insignia to create a very handsome and appropriate tribute of their dedicated military service to our nation.

The green background color plate features the insignia used by the Army Air Corps and Army Air Force. Uniform accoutrements plus aircrew wings are shown. Related text for these insignia is contained in the Army Air Force Insignia text section.

The uniform insignia of the U.S. Air Force follows on the next color plate. The plate begins with USAF hat insignia and then presents the currently authorized USAF aircrew wings. The wings are shown in order of receipt - basic, senior, and command/master/chief. The astronaut wings at the bottom of the plate depict three different specialties as representative examples with the astronaut designator.

The USAF missile badges begin the next color plate; occupational badges, both older and current styles, follow the missile badges. The older style security police qualification badge is shown in basic, senior, and chief versions to illustrate the three badge qualification levels available for all occupational badges. Current USAF badges are highly polished; for photography purposes to provide the most detail possible, either older silver oxide or "less polished" versions were used.

Additional special duty and qualification badges are shown on the next plate. Air Force rank insignia is shown on the following plate and provides representative samples of all officer and enlisted rank used by the Army Air Force and U.S. Air Force. Except for the three cloth insignia at the bottom of the plate, all rank is depicted in the metal version in the interest of space. The three cloth ranks depict styles used in the AAF, the USAF to 1997, and the USAF today. Note the difference in the USAF stripes -- today's stripes are bright white versus the previous edition of dull grey. Rank insignia is explained in both text and charts in other sections.

The next to last color plate shows the USAF aide insignia on the top line arranged and labeled in accordance with specific assignments. The Air Force Seal is presented in the center of the plate surrounded by U.S. Air Force Academy Insignia that is worn on the cadet uniform.

1782 Badge of Military Merit

DECORATIONS
AND SERVICE MEDALS

Since this book covers World War II forward, decorations and service medals for both the Army Air Force and United States Air Force are described in the following plates and each are referenced to more detailed descriptions. The listing is according to established USAF directives and precedence as of this writing (Note - World War II Campaign medals/ribbons, the Multinational Force Observers and the Inter-American Defense Board medal/ribbons, and foreign service ribbons should be worn in the order earned).

Unit citations that may have been earned as a member of the AAF are listed according to precedence of USAF, (realizing that unit citations according to Army regulations for AAF personnel were worn on the right chest) . If two medals are listed with similar requirements for AAF and USAF, they are shown with USAF medal having precedence. (i.e. Airman's Medal and Soldier's Medal).

This listing does not preclude the award of other service decorations to Air Force personnel. As I have seen during my examination of hundreds of separation papers and after many personal conversations with veterans of all periods, there have been many variations of awards of decorations and attachments that are not reflected in regulations of

the periods, such as World War II, Korea, and Vietnam. The criteria listed is in succinct form from USAF regulations (both current and older regulations). It should be noted that service requirements for certain medals are waived if an individual is wounded or killed. While awards and decorations from the other services may be worn, they are not included

The Andre Medal awarded to patriots Van Wert, Paulding and Williams by Continental Congress in 1780.

here. More detailed information can be obtained from both current USAF regulations and AAF/USAF regulations from 1941 to present day.

All decorations from the Army Distinguished Service Cross to and including the USAF Achievement Medal are authorized bronze oak leaf clusters to denote additional awards and silver oak leaf clusters to denote 5 additional awards.

The USAF Good Conduct Medal also uses oak leaf clusters to denote additional awards while the Army Good Conduct Medal uses bronze or silver knots (loops) to denote the total number of awards. Campaign medals use bronze stars to denote single campaign credits and silver stars to denote 5 campaign credits. Other medals and ribbons generally subscribe to these attachments; exceptions are noted in the description of the particular award.

Recently the Department of Defense has authorized Air Force personnel to wear the United Nations ribbon for the particular UN mission in which they participated. This is a change from previous guidance which only allowed the UN Korean Service ribbon for Korean veterans and a standard blue and white ribbon (UNSTO) ribbon for all other missions. The new change still restricts personnel to wearing only one UN ribbon and requires the use of bronze stars to indicate participation in other UN missions. Lonny Borts' book United Nations Medals and Missions is an excellent source for additional information on all UN medals .

Medals of Honor

MEDAL OF HONOR (AIR FORCE)

The Air Force design of the Medal of Honor was established by Congress on July 6, 1960 and presented to all Air Force recipients of the MOH on or after November 1, 1965. Criteria for awarding is the same as the Medal of Honor for the Army, "conspicuous gallantry and intrepidity at the risk of life above and beyond the call of duty." Each recommendation for the Medal of Honor must incontestably prove that the self sacrifice or personal bravery involved conspicuous risk of life.

The first recipient of the Medal of Honor - Air Force Design was Major Bernard F. Fisher on January 19, 1967 for his heroic actions in rescuing a fellow pilot who had crash landed on a landing strip in the A Shau Valley on March 10, 1966. Airman First Class John L. Levitow was the first USAF enlisted person to receive the Medal of Honor - Air Force Design; he was awarded the MOH for saving his AC-47 gunship and crew in Vietnam. Five airmen received the Medal of Honor during the Vietnam War. It is a five-pointed star within a green laurel wreath; laurel and oak are contained within each point of the star. The Statue of Liberty head is in the center of the medal. The star is suspended from a likeness of the Air Force Coat of Arms which is below a bar with the word "VALOR." The ribbon is twenty four inches long and contains 13 white stars in the center of the pad from which the medal hangs. The nation's highest award for valor for Air Force personnel should be referred to as the "Medal of Honor —Air Force design," not as the Air Force Medal of Honor.

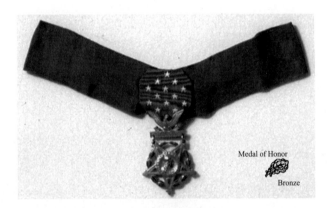

Medal of Honor

Bronze

MEDAL OF HONOR (ARMY)

The Medal of Honor (Army design) was presented to all AAF and USAF recipients of the MOH previous to the establishment of the MOH (Air Force design). Awarded for conspicuous gallantry and intrepidity at the risk of life above and beyond the call of duty. It was instituted in 1862. The 1996 Defense Authorization Act allowed reconsideration for the Medal of Honor for World War II veterans who received valor decorations but who could be eligible for this award. The first Army Medals of Honor were presented to five Union soldiers involved in the historic Great Locomotive Chase in the Civil War which involved an attempt to destroy the railroad between Chattanooga and Atlanta. The first Air Force person to receive the Medal of Honor was Captain Edward (Eddie) V. Rickenbacker of the U.S. Army Air Service who on September 25, 1918 shot down two aircraft when he attacked five fighters and two observation aircraft over France. The first AAF person to receive the Medal of Honor was Lieutenant Colonel James (Jimmy) H. Doolittle for his raid on Tokyo on April 18, 1942. There were 14 Medal of Honor winners from the Eighth Air Force during World War II and 4 awardees from the Ploesti oil field raids in August 1943 -- the most awarded for any single event in Air Force History. The first Medal of Honor awarded in the Korean War was to Major Louis J. Sebille who was killed on August 21, 1951 when he continued to attack enemy troops in his heavily damaged aircraft. Major Charles J. Loring, Jr. was the last USAF person to receive the Army Medal of Honor; as the flight leader of the 80th Fighter-Bomber Squadron, he received the award posthumously for flying his disabled F-80 aircraft into an enemy artillery position on Sniper Ridge during the Korean War, thus putting it out of action and protecting UN ground troops

The Medal of Honor is a five-pointed star with a green oak leaf within each point of the star and has a green laurel wreath encircling the center of the star. The Greek goddess Minerva, goddess of wisdom, is in the center of the star encircled by the inscription UNITED STATES OF AMERICA. The star is suspended from a bar with the word VALOR inscribed upon it and with an eagle sitting atop grasping both arrows and laurel leaves. The ribbon is a light blue neckband twenty four inches long containing 13 white stars in the center of the pad.

1862

Plate 1. MEDALS OF HONOR

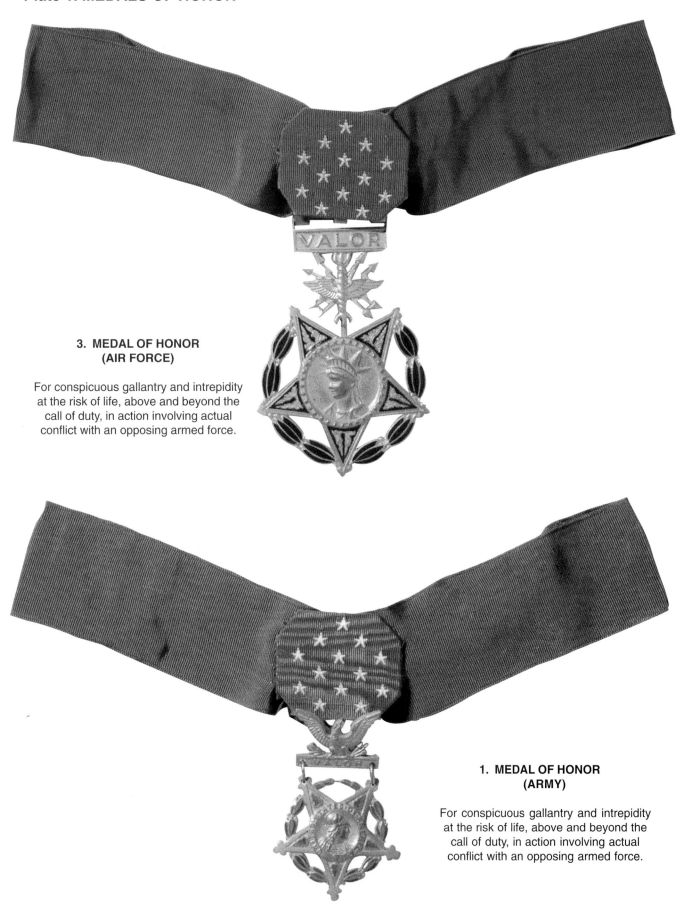

3. MEDAL OF HONOR
(AIR FORCE)

For conspicuous gallantry and intrepidity at the risk of life, above and beyond the call of duty, in action involving actual conflict with an opposing armed force.

1. MEDAL OF HONOR
(ARMY)

For conspicuous gallantry and intrepidity at the risk of life, above and beyond the call of duty, in action involving actual conflict with an opposing armed force.

Plate 2. U.S. Personal Decorations - Sheet 1

3. Air Force Cross (pg 82)

4. Distinguished Service Cross (pg 82)

5. Defense Distinguished Service Medal (pg 83)

6. Air Force Distinguished Service Medal (pg 83)

7. Army Distinguished Service Medal (pg 84)

8. Silver Star (pg 84)

9. Defense Superior Service Medal (pg 85)

10. Legion Of Merit (pg 85)

11. Dist. Flying Cross (pg 86)

12. Airman's Medal (pg 86)

13. Soldier's Medal (pg 87)

14. Bronze Star Medal (pg 87)

Plate 2. U.S. Personal Decorations - Sheet 2

15. Purple Heart
(pg 88)

16. Defense Meritorious
Service Medal (pg 89)

17. Meritorious
Service Medal
(pg 89)

18. Air Medal
(pg 90)

19. Aerial
Achievement
Medal (pg 90)

20. Joint Service
Commendation
Medal (pg 91)

21. Air Force
Commendation
Medal (pg 91)

22. Army
Commendation
Medal (pg 92)

23. Joint Service
Achievement Medal
(pg 92)

24. Air Force
Achievement
Medal (pg 93)

25. Air Force Presidential
Unit Citation (pg 93)

26. Joint Meritorious Unit
Award (pg 94)

27. Air Force Outstanding Unit
Award (pg 94)

28. Air Force Organiza-
tional Excellence Award
(pg 95)

29. Prisoner Of War
Medal (pg 95)

Plate 3. U.S. Special Service, Good Conduct, and Reserve Awards

30. Combat Readiness Medal (pg96)

31. Air Force Good Conduct Medal (pg97)

32. Army Good Conduct Medal (pg97)

33. Air Reserve Forces Meritorious Service Medal (pg98)

34. Outstanding Airman of the Year Ribbon (pg98)

35. Air Force Recognition Ribbon (pg98)

36. American Defense Service Medal (pg99)

37. Women's Army Corps Service Medal (pg99)

38. American Campaign Medal (pg99)

39. European-African-Middle Eastern Campaign Medal (pg101)

40. Asiatic-Pacific Campaign Medal (pg102)

41. World War II Victory Medal (pg103)

42. Army of Occupation Medal (pg103)

Plate 4. U.S. Service Medals

43. Medal for Humane Action (pg104)

44. National Defense Service Medal (pg104)

45. Korean Service Medal (pg105)

47. Antarctica Service Medal (pg106)

48. Armed Forces Expeditionary Medal (pg106)

49. Vietnam Service Medal (pg107)

49. Southwest Asia Service Medal (pg108)

50. Armed Forces Service Medal (pg108)

51. Humanitarian Service Medal (pg109)

52. Outstanding Volunteer Service Medal (pg109)

53. Overseas Service Ribbon (Short Tour)(pg111)

54. Overseas Service Ribbon (Long Tour) (pg111)

55. Air Force Longevity Service Award (pg111)

56. Armed Forces Reserve Medal (pg110)

57. NCO Prof.Military Education Graduate

58. Basic Military Training Honor Graduate Ribbon

59. Air Force Small Arms Expert Marksmanship

60. Air Force Training Ribbon (pg112)

Plate 5. Foreign Decorations and Non-U.S. Service Awards

61. Philippine Defense Medal (pg113)

62. Philippine Liberation medal (pg113)

63. Philippine Independence Medal (pg114)

64. RVN Gallantry Cross (pg114)

65. Philippine Presidential Unit Citation (pg115)

66. Korean Presidential Unit Citation (pg115)

67. Republic of Vietnam Gallantry Cross Unit Citation (pg115)

68. Republic of Vietnam Civil Actions Unit Citation (pg115)

69. United Nations Service Medal (Korea) (pg116)

70. United Nations Medal (Observer Medal) (pg116)

80.Multinational Force and Observers Medal (pg117)

81. Inter-American Defense Board Medal (pg118)

82. RVN Campaign Medal (pg118)

83. Saudi Arabian Medal for the Liberation of Kuwait (pg119)

85. Kuwaiti Medal for the Liberation of Kuwait (pg119)

86. NATO Medal (pg111)

Plate 6. AAF and USAF Patches

Army Air
Force

5th Air Force

8th Air
Force

15th Air
Force

14th Air Force

Airborne
Troop Carrier

AAF Aviation
Cadet

AAF Armament
Specialist

AAF
Engineering
Specialist

AAF Weather
Specialist

AAF
Communications
Specialist

AAF
Photography
Specialist

Meritorious Unit   Ruptured Duck

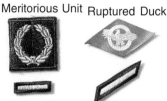
Overseas Svc.   Service Stripe
Bar

Strategic Air
Command

Tactical Air
Command

Air Combat
Command

Air Education & Train.
Command

Headquarters
Command

337th
Bombardment
Squadron

441st
Bombardment
Squadron

3535th Navigator
Training Wing

1st Combat
Evaluation Group

320th
Bombardment Wing

Navigator Training
Class 70-16

Strategic Air
Command Bombing
Competition

B-52 100 Missions

Aerospace Defense
Command

Pilot Training
Class 70-01

356th Navigator
Training Squadron

B-52

USAF Retired

96th
Bombardment
Wing

USAF Academy Cadet
Squadron 28

71

Examples of Air Force Awards Displays World War II to Present

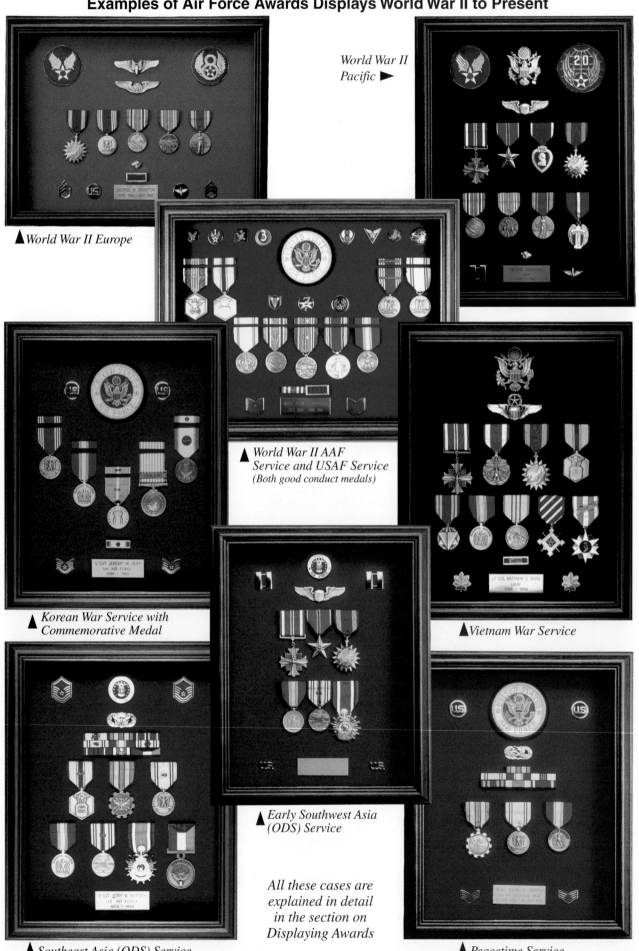

World War II
Pacific ▶

▲*World War II Europe*

▲ *World War II AAF*
Service and USAF Service
(Both good conduct medals)

▲ *Korean War Service with*
Commemorative Medal

▲*Vietnam War Service*

▲ *Early Southwest Asia*
(ODS) Service

All these cases are
explained in detail
in the section on
Displaying Awards

▲ *Southeast Asia (ODS) Service*

▲ *Peacetime Service*

Plate 8 AAF Uniform and Wing Insignia

AAF Aviation Cadet Hat device

Army Officer Hat Insignia

Army Enlisted Hat Insignia

Officers US collar Insignia

WW2 Honorable Discharge Pin

Army Aviation Officer Branch Insignia

Army Warrant Officer Hat Insignia

Enlisted US Collar Insignia

Gold Star Lapel Pin

Enlisted Aviation Branch

Pilot Wings

Navigator Wings

Bombardier Wings

Enlisted Aircrew Member Wings

Aerial Gunner Wings

Flight Engineer Wings

Technical Observer Wings

Liaison Pilot Wings

Combat Observer Wings

Service Pilot Wings

Glider Pilot Wings

Airship Pilot Wings

Balloon Pilot Wings

Women's Air Service Pilot Wings

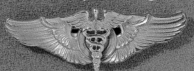

AAF Flight Surgeon Wings (Gold)

AAF Flight Surgeon Wings (Silver)

Plate 9 USAF Uniform and Wing Insignia

USAF Women's Officer Hat Device

USAF Retired Pin

USAF Officer's US Collar Insignia

Male Officer's Hat Device

USAF Enlisted Man's Collar Insignia

USAF Enlisted Man's Hat Device

Pilot Wings

Senior Pilot Wings

Command Pilot Wings

Navigator (Aircraft Observer) Wings

Senior Navigator Wings

Master Navigator Wings

Non-Rated Officer Aircrew Wings

Senior Non-Rated Officer Aircrew

Chief Non-Rated Officer Aircrew

USAF Flight Surgeon Wings

Senior Flight Surgeon Wings

Chief Flight Surgeon Wings

USAF Flight Nurse Wings

Senior Flight Nurse Wings

Chief Flight Nurse Wings

Pilot Astronaut Wings

Senior Flight Surgeon Astronaut Wings

Master Navigator Astronaut Wings

Enlisted Aircrew Member Wings

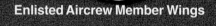
Senior Enlisted Aircrew Wings

Chief Enlisted Aircrew Wings

74

Plate 10 USAF Missile and Occupational Badges

Missile/ Missile Maintenance   Senior Missile/ Missile Maintenance   Master Missile/ Missile Maintenance   Missile Operator/ Missile   Senior Missile Operator/Missile   Master Missile Operator/Missile

Security Police   Senior Security Police   Chief Security Police

Operations Support   Weapons Controller   Air Traffic Control   Command and Control   Space/Missile

Intelligence Badge   Meterorologist Badge   Communications-Electronics Maint.   Supply/Fuels (Old)   Chief Supply/Fuels (New)

Maintenance   Transportation   Logistics   Civil Engineer   Explosive Ordnance

Communications   Services   Band   Public Affairs   Historian

Manpower and Personnel   Information Management   Security Police Qualification   Law Enforcement   Judge Advocate

Christian Chaplain   Jewish Chaplain   Buddhist Chaplain   Muslim Chaplain   Paralegal   Chaplain Service Support

Acquisition and Financial Management   Physician   Medical Service   Biomedical Science   Nurse   Dental   Veterinarian   Medical Technologist

Plate 11 USAF Recruiting Badges

USAF Recruiter (New)	USAF Recruiter	Senior	Senior (Numbered)	Master

USAFR Recruiter	USAFR Century Club (100)	USAFR Century Club (200)	USAFR Master

USAFR Staff Recruiting	USAFR Staff Century Club (100)	USAFR Staff Century Club (200)	USAFR Master Staff

USAFR Senior Recruiter	USAFR Senior Century Club	USAFR Senior Century Club (200)	USAFR Master Senior

USAFR Medical Recruiter	USAFR Medical Century Club	USAFR Medical Century Club (200)	USAFR Master Medical

ANG Recruiter	ANG Senior Longevity	ANG Master Longevity	ANG Rookie of the Year	ANG Master

Plate 12 Special Qualification Badges

Presidential Service Badge

Sec of Def ID Badge

JCS ID Badge

USAFA Permanent Professor

Basic Parachutist

Senior Parachutist

Master Parachutist

Basic Parachutist (Old)

Senior Parachutist (Old)

Master Parachutist (Old)

Combat Crewmember

Combat Control Team

Pararescue

Security Police ID

AETC Instructor

ATC Instructor

ATC Master Instructor

AETC Master Instructor

Fire Chief

Deputy Fire Chief

Assistant Fire Chief

Firefighter

Plate 13 USAF Officer and Enlisted Rank Insignia

2 Lt

1 Lt

Capt

Major

Lt Col

Col

Brig Gen.

Maj Gen

Lt Gen

General

General of the
Air   Force

Amn

Amn 1/C

Sgt/Sr Amn

S/Sgt

T/Sgt

M/Sgt
(w/diamond-
1st Sgt)

Amn

Amn 1/C

Sr Amn

M/Sgt

M/Sgt (1st Sgt)

S/MSgt (Old)

S/MSt

C/MSgt (Old)

C/MSgt

CMSAF

Flight
Officer

Warrant
Officer W-1

Chief Warrant
Officer W-2

Chief Warrant
Officer W-3

Chief Warrant
Officer W-4

Technician
4th Grade

Technical
Sergeant

C/MSgt (New)
1st Sgt

Plate 14 Special Qualification Badges

Military Aide Insignia

Junior AFROTC Instructor

Military Aviator Badge

USAF Band Hat Device

USAFA Hat Insignia

USAFA Bulldog Badge

USAF Seal

USAFA Parachutist Badge

USAFA Superint.'s Pin

USAFA Dean/ Athletic Pin

USAFA Comm./ Ath. Pin

USAFA Comm./ Dean's Pin

USAFA Dean's Pin

USAFA Comm.'s Pin

USAFA Athletic Pin

Air Assault Badge

USAFA Cadet Nav. Instr. Wings

USAFA Cadet Sr. Nav. Instructor

USAFA Recondo Pin

USAFA Cadet Flight Wings

USAFA Cadet Inst. Pilot Wings

USAFA Cadet Sr. Inst. Pilot Wings

U.S. Air Force
Correct Order Of Ribbon Wear
(Left Breast)

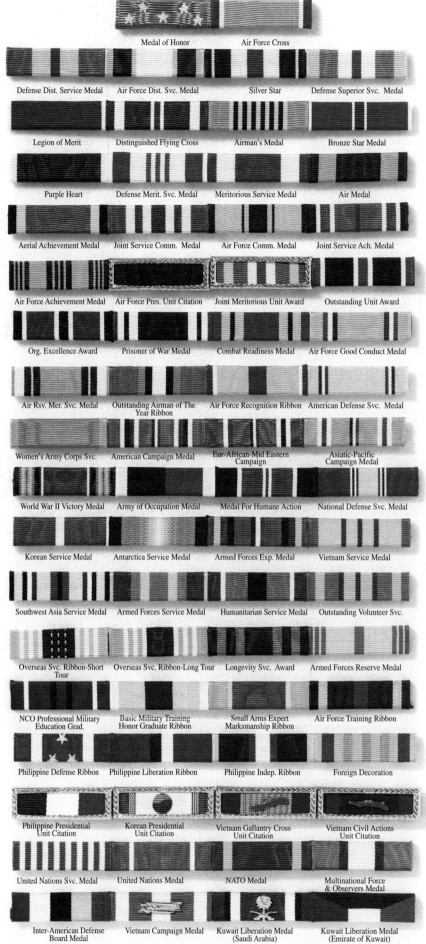

Medal of Honor   Air Force Cross

Defense Dist. Service Medal   Air Force Dist. Svc. Medal   Silver Star   Defense Superior Svc. Medal

Legion of Merit   Distinguished Flying Cross   Airman's Medal   Bronze Star Medal

Purple Heart   Defense Merit. Svc. Medal   Meritorious Service Medal   Air Medal

Aerial Achievement Medal   Joint Service Comm. Medal   Air Force Comm. Medal   Joint Service Ach. Medal

Air Force Achievement Medal   Air Force Pres. Unit Citation   Joint Meritorious Unit Award   Outstanding Unit Award

Org. Excellence Award   Prisoner of War Medal   Combat Readiness Medal   Air Force Good Conduct Medal

Air Rsv. Mer. Svc. Medal   Outstanding Airman of The Year Ribbon   Air Force Recognition Ribbon   American Defense Svc. Medal

Women's Army Corps Svc.   American Campaign Medal   Eur-African-Mid Eastern Campaign   Asiatic-Pacific Campaign Medal

World War II Victory Medal   Army of Occupation Medal   Medal For Humane Action   National Defense Svc. Medal

Korean Service Medal   Antarctica Service Medal   Armed Forces Exp. Medal   Vietnam Service Medal

Southwest Asia Service Medal   Armed Forces Service Medal   Humanitarian Service Medal   Outstanding Volunteer Svc.

Overseas Svc. Ribbon-Short Tour   Overseas Svc. Ribbon-Long Tour   Longevity Svc. Award   Armed Forces Reserve Medal

NCO Professional Military Education Grad.   Basic Military Training Honor Graduate Ribbon   Small Arms Expert Marksmanship Ribbon   Air Force Training Ribbon

Philippine Defense Ribbon   Philippine Liberation Ribbon   Philippine Indep. Ribbon   Foreign Decoration

Philippine Presidential Unit Citation   Korean Presidential Unit Citation   Vietnam Gallantry Cross Unit Citation   Vietnam Civil Actions Unit Citation

United Nations Svc. Medal   United Nations Medal   NATO Medal   Multinational Force & Observers Medal

Inter-American Defense Board Medal   Vietnam Campaign Medal   Kuwait Liberation Medal (Saudi Arabia)   Kuwait Liberation Medal (Emirate of Kuwait)

	Medal of Honor Bronze	Air Force Cross Silver Bronze	
Defense Distinguished Service Medal Bronze	Air Force Distinguished Service Medal Silver Bronze	Silver Star Silver Bronze	Defense Superior Service Medal Silver Bronze
Legion of Merit Silver Bronze	Distinguished Flying Cross Silver Bronze	Airman's Medal Bronze	Bronze Star Medal Bronze Silver Bronze
Purple Heart Silver Bronze	Defense Meritorious Service Medal Silver Bronze	Meritorious Service Medal Silver Bronze	Air Medal Silver Bronze
Aerial Achievement Medal Silver Bronze	Joint Svc. Commendation Medal Bronze Silver Bronze	Air Force Commendation Medal Bronze Silver Bronze	Joint Svc. Achievement Medal Silver Bronze
Air Force Achievement Medal Bronze Silver Bronze	Air Force Presidential Unit Citation Silver Bronze	Joint Meritorious Unit Award Silver Bronze	Outstanding Unit Award Bronze Silver Bronze
Organizational Excellence Award Bronze Silver Bronze	Prisoner of War Medal Silver Bronze	Combat Readiness Medal Silver Bronze	Air Force Good Conduct Medal Silver Bronze
Air Reserve Forces Meritorious Service Medal Silver Bronze	Outstanding Airman of the Year Ribbon Bronze Silver Bronze	Air Force Recognition Ribbon Silver Bronze	American Defense Service Medal Bronze
Women's Army Corps Service Medal None	American Campaign Medal Bronze	European-African-Middle Eastern Campaign Bronze Silver Bronze	Asiatic-Pacific Campaign Medal Bronze Silver Bronze
World War II Victory Medal None	Army of Occupation Medal Gold Airplane	Medal For Humane Action None	National Defense Service Medal Bronze
Korean Service Medal Bronze Silver Bronze	Antarctica Service Medal Bronze, Gold, or Silver	Armed Forces Expeditionary Medal Silver Bronze	Vietnam Service Medal Silver Bronze
Southwest Asia Service Medal Bronze	Armed Forces Service Medal Silver Bronze	Humanitarian Service Medal Silver Bronze	Outstanding Volunteer Service Medal Silver Bronze
Overseas Service Ribbon - Short Tour Silver Bronze	Overseas Service Ribbon - Long Tour Silver Bronze	Longevity Service Award Ribbon Silver Bronze	Armed Forces Reserve Medal Bronze, Silver, Gold Hourglass Bronze
NCO Prof. Mil. Education Grad. Ribbon Silver Bronze	Basic Military Training Honor Graduate Ribbon None	Small Arms Expert Marksmanship Ribbon Bronze	Air Force Training Ribbon Silver Bronze
Philippine Defense Ribbon Bronze	Philippine Liberation Ribbon Bronze	Philippine Independence Ribbon None	Foreign Decoration As specified by the Awarding Government
Philippine Republic Presidential Unit Citation Bronze	Republic of Korea Presidential Unit Citation None	Vietnam Gallantry Cross Unit Citation Bronze Palm	Vietnam Civil Actions Unit Citation Bronze Palm
United Nations Service Medal None	United Nations Medal Bronze	NATO Medal Bronze	Multinational Force & Observers Medal Bronze Numeral
Inter-American Defense Board Medal Gold	Republic of Vietnam Campaign Medal Silver Date Bar	Kuwait Liberation Medal (Saudi Arabia) Gold Palm Tree	Kuwait Liberation Medal (Emirate of Kuwait) None

 = **Bronze Oak Leaf Cluster**
Denotes second and subsequent awards of a Joint Service decoration or unit citation

 = **Silver Oak Leaf Cluster**
Worn in lieu of five bronze oak leaf clusters

 = **Bronze Service Star**
Denotes second and subsequent awards of a service award or participation in a campaign or major operation

= **Silver Service Star**
Worn in lieu of five gold or bronze service stars

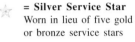 = **Bronze Letter "V"**
Awarded for distinguished actions in combat

= **Bronze Letter "M"**
Denotes reservists mobilized and called to active duty

 = **Bronze Arrowhead**
Denotes participation in parachute, glider or amphibious landing or assault

 = **Antarctica Disk**
Denotes personnel who "winter-over" on the Antarctic continent

 = **Bronze Numeral**
Denotes total number of strike/flight awards of the Air Medals and other awards

 = **Berlin Airlift Device**

 = **Palm**

 = **Date Bar, Silver**

 = **Hourglass**
Issued for each succeeding award of the Armed Forces Reserve Medal

AIR FORCE CROSS

<u>Service</u>: Air Force
<u>Instituted</u>: 1960
<u>Criteria</u>: Extraordinary heroism in action against an enemy of the U.S. or while serving with friendly foreign forces
<u>Devices</u>: Bronze, silver oak leaf cluster

Authorized on November 1, 1965 for extraordinary heroism while engaged in a military action against an enemy of the United States; previous to the effective date of July 6, 1960, awarded individuals received the Army Distinguished Service Cross (DSC) except for several World War II veterans who had been approved for the DSC but had never received it. It is awarded for heroic actions not justifying the Medal of Honor and is presented in the name of the President. The first award of the Air Force Cross was made posthumously to Major Rudolf Anderson, Jr. who was shot down and killed over Cuba during the Cuban missile crisis while flying a U-2 aircraft. The first living enlisted man to receive the Air Force Cross was Sgt. Duane D. Hackney who received it for rescuing a downed Air Force pilot in Vietnam. T/Sgt Tim Wilkinson, an Air Force pararescueman, as of this writing, is the most recent USAF person to receive the Air Force Cross; he received his award for his heroic actions during the October 1993 firefight in Mogadishu, Somalia when, despite injuries and intense enemy fire, he treated injured Army helicopter crews and injured Army rangers. The design of the Air Force Cross medal and ribbon is based on the design of the Army Distinguished Service Cross. The medal is a bronze cross containing a gold-plated American bald eagle with wings against a cloud formation encircled by a green laurel wreath. Awardee's name may be engraved on the reverse. The blue in the center of the ribbon is a lighter shade than that of the DSC. Additional awards are denoted by attaching an oak leaf cluster to the medal and ribbon.

DISTINGUISHED SERVICE CROSS (ARMY)

<u>Service</u>: Army
<u>Instituted</u>: 1918
<u>Criteria</u>: Extraordinary heroism in action against an enemy of the U.S. or while serving with friendly foreign forces
<u>Devices</u>: Bronze, silver oak leaf cluster
<u>Notes</u>: 100 copies of earlier design cross issued with a European-style (unedged) ribbon ("French Cut")

Authorized by Congress on July 9, 1918. Awarded for extraordinary heroism against an armed enemy but of a level not justifying the award of the Medal of Honor. It may be awarded to both civilians and military serving in any capacity with the Army who distinguish themselves by heroic actions in combat. The act or acts of heroism must be so notable and have involved risk of life so extraordinary as to set the individual apart from his comrades. The medal had been initially proposed for award to qualifying members of the American Expeditionary Forces in Europe during World War I but was authorized permanently by Congress in the Appropriations Act of 1918. While DSCs were originally numbered, the practice was discontinued during World War II. The first American Expeditionary Force Air Service member to receive the DSC was Lieutenant Paul Baer on March 11, 1918. In 1934 the DSC was authorized to be presented to holders of the Certificate of Merit which had been discontinued in 1918 when the Distinguished Service Medal was established. USAF members continued to receive this decoration after the Air Force became a separate service in 1947 and until the Air Force Cross was authorized in 1965. The medal is in the shape of a cross with an eagle centered on the cross. The eagle represents the United States and the oak leaves surrounding the eagle symbolize strength and courage. On the reverse is a plaque inscribed with the words "FOR VALOR." The ribbon is primarily a deep blue with white and red edges; the blue stands for high purpose, the white for purity, and the red for sacrifice. Additional awards are denoted by the placement of oak leaf clusters on the medal drape and ribbon bar.

DEFENSE DISTINGUISHED SERVICE MEDAL

Silver   Bronze

Service: All Services (by Secretary of Defense)

Instituted: 1970

Criteria: Exceptionally meritorious service to the United States while assigned to a Joint Activity in a position of unique and great responsibility

Devices: Army/Air Force/ Navy/Marine Corps: bronze & silver oak leaf cluster; Coast Guard: gold, silver star

Notes: Coast Guard uses gold star device since the oak leaf cluster may not be worn on its uniform

Authorized on July 9, 1970 and awarded to military officers for exceptionally meritorious service while assigned to a Department of Defense joint activity. The Secretary of Defense is the awarding authority for the medal, usually awarded to the most senior officers. Examples of assignments that may allow qualification for this medal are: Chairman, Joint Chiefs of Staff; Chiefs and Vice Chiefs of the Military Services, including the Commandant and Assistant Commandant of the Marine Corps; and Commanders and Vice Commanders of Unified and Specified Commands. It may also be awarded to other senior officers who serve in positions of great responsibility, or to an officer whose direct and individual contributions to national security or defense are also recognized as being so exceptional in scope and value as to be equivalent to contributions normally associated with positions encompassing broader responsibilities. Oak leaf clusters are the appropriate attachments for Air Force personnel for subsequent awards.

The medal depicts an American bald eagle with wings spread and the United States shield on its breast; the eagle is superimposed on a light blue pentagon and is surrounded by a gold circle that has thirteen stars in the upper half and a laurel wreath in the lower half. On the back of the medal is the inscription "FROM THE SECRETARY OF DEFENSE TO...FOR DISTINGUISHED SERVICE." Space is provided between the "TO" and "FOR" for engraving of the recipient's name.

DISTINGUISHED SERVICE MEDAL (AIR FORCE)

Silver   Bronze

Service: Air Force

Instituted: 1960

Criteria: Exceptionally meritorious service to the United States Government in a duty of great responsibility

Devices: Bronze, silver oak leaf cluster

Notes: Original design was modified and used as the Airman's Medal

The Air Force Distinguished Service Medal was authorized by Congress on July 6, 1960; it evolved from the Army Distinguished Service Medal authorized in 1918. The medal is awarded for exceptionally meritorious service to the U.S. in a duty of great responsibility; the term "great responsibility" denotes the success of a major operation or program attributed to the proper exercise of authority and judgement. This is the highest peacetime Air Force decoration awarded. It is presented to all recipients who are awarded this decoration on or after November 1, 1965; AAF and USAF personnel who were awarded this decoration prior to this date received the Army version. The Air Force Distinguished Service Medal is rarely awarded to officers below the rank of Brigadier General. The medal should be referred to as "Distinguished Service Medal - Air Force design." Major General Osmond J. Ritland, Air Force Systems Command, was the first recipient of the Air Force Distinguished Service Medal on November 30, 1965 for his efforts as Deputy Commander for Manned Space Flight. Subsequent awards are denoted by the attachment of an oak leaf cluster to the medal and ribbon. Individuals who have received both the Army DSM and the Air Force DSM should wear both of the medals/ribbons with the Air Force version taking precedence. The medal is a blue stone centered within 13 gold rays, each separated by 13 white stars. The recipient's name may be engraved on the back of the medal.

DISTINGUISHED SERVICE MEDAL (ARMY)

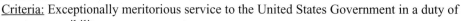

Distinguished Service Medal

Bronze

Service: Army
Instituted: 1918
Criteria: Exceptionally meritorious service to the United States Government in a duty of great responsibility
Devices: Bronze, silver oak leaf cluster
Notes: Originally issued with European (unedged) ribbon ("French Cut")

        Authorized by Congress on July 9, 1918 for exceptionally meritorious service to the United States while serving in a duty of great responsiblity with the U.S. Army. It was originally intended for award for qualifying actions during wartime but was authorized for qualifying actions during wartime or peacetime. As this country's highest award for meritorious service or achievement, it has been awarded to both military and civilians, foreign and domestic. The first American to receive this medal was General John J. Pershing, commanding general of the American Expeditionary Forces during World War I, on October 12, 1918. Individuals who had received the Certificate of Merit before its disestablishment in 1918 were authorized to receive the DSM. The Army DSM is seldom awarded to civilians and personnel below the rank of Brigadier General. The reverse of the medal contains a scroll for engraving of the recipient's name. Subsequent awards are denoted by the attachment of a bronze oak leaf cluster to the medal and ribbon. The medal is a circular design containing the US Coat of Arms encircled by a blue ring with the inscription "FOR DISTINGUISHED SERVICE MCMXVII." In the center of the reverse of the medal amidst several flags and weapons is a blank scroll for engraving the awardee's name.

SILVER STAR

Silver Star

Silver   Bronze

Service: All Services (originally Army only)
Instituted: 1932
Criteria: Gallantry in action against an armed enemy of the United States or while serving with friendly foreign forces
Devices: Army/Air Force: bronze, silver oak leaf cluster; Navy/Marine Corps/Coast Guard: gold, silver star
Notes: Derived from the 3/16" silver "Citation Star" previously worn on Army campaign medals

        Authorized on July 9,1918 with no initial qualifying date established, it is awarded for gallantry in action against an enemy of the United States while engaged in military operations involving conflict against an opposing armed force in which the United States is not a belligerent party. The degree of gallantry required, while of a high degree, is less than that required for the Medal of Honor or Air Force Cross. Gallantry in action means heroism of a high degree including risk of life. When originally authorized and until its present form was approved in 1932 by the Secretary of War, the Silver Star was known as the "Citation Star." The Citation Star was 3/16th inch in diameter and was affixed to the campaign medal for which it was awarded; it was primarily affixed to the World War I Victory Medal. The first Silver Star was presented to General Douglas MacArthur. On December 15, 1942 Congress authorized the award for civilians serving with the armed forces who met the stated criteria specified in the initial regulation. Additional awards are denoted by attaching either bronze or silver oak leaf clusters to the medal and ribbon. The medal is a small (3/16th inch diameter) silver star within a wreath centered on a larger star of gold-colored metal. The reverse contains the inscription "FOR GALLANTRY IN ACTION."

DEFENSE SUPERIOR SERVICE MEDAL

Silver   Bronze

Service: All Services (by Secretary of Defense)
Instituted: 1970
Criteria: Superior meritorious service to the United States while assigned to a Joint Activity in a position of significant responsibility
Devices: Army/Air Force/ Navy/Marine Corps: bronze, silver oak leaf cluster ; Coast Guard: gold, silver star
Notes: Coast Guard uses gold star device since the oak leaf cluster may not be worn on its uniform

Authorized on February 6, 1976 by an executive order signed by President Gerald R. Ford. Awarded by the Secretary of Defense to any member of the armed forces for superior meritorious service after February 6, 1976 in a position of significant responsibility while assigned to a DOD joint activity, including the Office of the Secretary of Defense, the Joint Chiefs of Staff, and specified and unified commands. The medal was created to provide recognition to those assigned to joint duty on a level equivalent to that recognition provided by the Legion of Merit. Prior to establishment of the Defense Superior Service Medal, the Office of the Secretary of Defense had to provide recognition through equivalent awards that were approved through individual service channels. Although it was established as equivalent to the Legion of Merit, its precedence is before the Legion of Merit when both are worn. Oak leaf clusters are the appropriate attachments for additional awards to Air Force personnel. The medal depicts a silver American eagle with outstretched wings and the United States shield on its breast and grasping in its talons three crossed silver arrows; the eagle is encircled on the top half by a silver arc of 13 stars and on the bottom half by a laurel wreath.

LEGION OF MERIT

Legion of Merit

Silver   Bronze

Service: All Services
Instituted: 1942
Criteria: Exceptionally meritorious conduct in the performance of outstanding services to the United States
Devices: Army/Air Force: bronze, silver oak leaf cluster; Navy/Marine Corps/Coast Guard: bronze letter "V" (for valor), gold, silver star
Notes: Issued in four degrees (Legionnaire, Officer, Commander & Chief Commander) to foreign nationals

Authorized by Congress on July 20, 1942 for award to members of the Armed Forces of the United States for exceptionally meritorious conduct in the performance of outstanding service. Superior performance of normal duties will not alone justify award of this decoration. It is not awarded for heroism but rather service and achievement while performing duties in a key positon of responsibility. It may be presented to foreign personnel but is not authorized for presentment to civilian personnel. There are four degrees of this decoration that are awarded to foreign personnel only (Chief Commander, Commander, Officer, and Legionnaire). The first two degrees are comparable in rank to the Distinguished Service Medal and are usually awarded to heads of state and to commanders of armed forces, respectively. The last two degrees are comparable in rank to the award of the Legion of Merit to U.S. service members. While there has been no stated policy in the Air Force as to what ranks can be awarded this decoration, it is usually not awarded to officer ranks below Colonel (O-6); while there are exceptions, there have been many instances where officers below the rank of Colonel have occupied equivalent positions of responsibility as an O-6 but have received the Meritorious Service Medal for similar levels of performance that warranted a Legion of Merit for the O-6. The Legion of Merit has often been used as an end of tour or retirement decoration for Colonels and above. The medal is not often presented to non-commissioned officers or junior officers. The medal is a five-rayed white enamel pronged star on a green wreath with crossed arrows. The cloud and stars of U.S. coat of arms are displayed in the center.

DISTINGUISHED FLYING CROSS

Silver   Bronze

Service: All Services
Instituted: 1926
Criteria: Heroism or extraordinary achievement while participating in aerial flight
Devices: Army/Air Force: bronze, silver oak leaf cluster; Navy/Marine Corps: bronze letter "V" (for valor), gold, silver star; Coast Guard: gold, silver star

     Authorized on July 2, 1926 and implemented with an executive order signed by President Calvin Coolidge on January 28, 1927. It is awarded to United States military personnel for heroism or extraordinary achievement that is clearly distinctive involving operations during aerial flight that are not routine. Captain Charles A. Lindbergh was the first recipient of the Distinguished Flying Cross on June 11, 1927 for his solo flight across the Atlantic. The Wright Brothers were awarded the DFC by an Act of Congress for their first manned flight at Kitty Hawk, North Carolina in 1903. Amelia Earhart became the only female civilian to be awarded the DFC when it was presented to her by the United States Army Air Corps in 1932 for her aerial exploits. Additional awards to Air Force personnel are denoted by the attachment of bronze and silver oak leaf clusters to the ribbon and medal. Note that unlike the Navy and Marine Corps, the V attachment is not used for the DFC for Air Force personnel. While the Distinguished Flying Cross was never intended to be an automatic award, the Army Air Force did use it in that capacity many times during World War II by awarding DFCs for specific number of sorties and flying hours in the combat theater. The front of the medal is a four-bladed propeller contained within a bronze cross suspended from a straight bar attached to the medal drape. The reverse is blank and provides space for the recipient's name and date of the award.

AIRMAN'S MEDAL

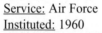

Airman's Medal

Bronze

Service: Air Force
Instituted: 1960
Criteria: Heroism involving voluntary risk of life under conditions other than those of actual conflict with an armed enemy
Devices: Bronze, silver oak leaf cluster
Notes: Derived from original design of Air Force Distinguished Service Medal

     Authorized on August 10, 1956 and instituted on July 6, 1960; the authorizing directive was an amendment to the directive creating the Soldier's Medal. The naming of the medal was obviously a carryover from the Soldier's medal and does not immediately make one aware of the significance of the act required to be awarded the decoration. Awarded for actions involving voluntary risk of life under conditions other than combat. A successful voluntary heroic act or the saving of a life is not essential to the award of this decoration. The first Airman's Medal was awarded to Captain John Burger on July 21, 1960 at McDill AFB, Tampa, Florida for saving a fellow airman's life by removing a live power line that laid across his body after having been severely shocked. Another example of the heroism required for award of the Airman's Medal was the bravery exhibited by Senior Airman Joe Sampson of Charleston AFB, South Carolina when he saved an Army jumpmaster's life at the risk of his own aboard a C-141 aircraft carrying Army paratroopers. After the jumpmaster's reserve parachute had extracted inadvertently and threatened to pull him out of the aircraft, Sr Amn Sampson, without hesitation, grabbed the jumpmaster and his chute and pulled him back into into the aircraft despite the tremendous forces of the airstream. Previously all USAF personnel qualifying for such an award were awarded the Soldier's Medal. The American bald eagle is depicted along with the Greek god Hermes, herald and messenger of other gods, on the face of the medal. The reverse contains space for engraving just below the inscription "For Valor."

SOLDIER'S MEDAL

Soldier's Medal

Silver   Bronze

Service: Army
Instituted: 1926
Criteria: Heroism not involving actual conflict with an armed enemy of the United States
Devices: Bronze, silver oak leaf cluster

Authorized by Congress on July 2, 1926 to a member of the Army, National Guard, or Reserves for heroism not involving actual conflict with an enemy. Would have been awarded to AAF/USAF personnel for qualifying actions prior to establishment of the Airman's Medal in 1960. The bronze octagonal medal has an eagle with raised wings and seven stars on its left and six stars and a spray of leaves on its right side. The reverse has a U.S. shield with sprays of laurel and oak in front of a scroll. The words "SOLDIER'S MEDAL" and "FOR VALOR" are inscribed on the reverse.

BRONZE STAR MEDAL

Bronze Star Medal

V

Bronze   Silver   Bronze

Service: All Services
Instituted: 1944
Criteria: Heroic or meritorious achievement or service not involving participation in aerial flight
Devices: Army/Air Force: bronze letter "V" (for valor), bronze, silver oak leaf cluster; Navy/Marine Corps/Coast Guard: bronze letter "V" (for valor), gold, silver star
Notes: Awarded to World War II holders of Army Combat Infantryman Badge or Combat Medical Badge

Authorized on February 4, 1944 and retroactive to December 7, 1941. May be awarded to individuals serving in any capacity with the Armed Forces of the United States for heroism in combat not involving aerial flight or for meritorious service. In September 1947 the Bronze Star Medal was authorized for all holders of either the Combat Infantryman's Badge (CIB) or the Combat Medical Badge (CMB) from December 7, 1941 to September 2, 1945. Some AAF personnel may have become eligible for this award if they participated in the Philippine Islands Campaign between December 7, 1941 and May 10, 1942 and if their service was on the island of Luzon or the Harbor Defenses in Corregidor and Bataan; they must have been awarded the Philippine Presidential Unit Citation to be awarded this decoration. Many World War II infantry veterans who had received either the CIB or CMB never knew that they were eligible to receive this medal since it was not listed on their records at discharge and they were not automatically notified of the blanket award. A "V" device is awarded if the medal was awarded for heroism in combat. The "V" device was approved in 1945 to clearly distinguish between awards of the medal for heroism in combat or for meritorious service; the "V" was initially only authorized for this medal until its use was expanded in 1966. Additional awards for Air Force personnel are denoted by the attachment of oak leaf clusters to the medal and ribbon. While an individual may receive more than one award of the Bronze Star with V, they are only authorized to display one; for example, an individual who receives two Bronze Star with Vs would have one V and 1 bronze oak leaf cluster on the medal drape/ribbon. The Medal is a five-pointed bronze star with a smaller star in the center (similar in design to the Silver Star Medal); the reverse contains the inscription "HEROIC OR MERITORIOUS ACHIEVEMENT" in a circular pattern.).

PURPLE HEART

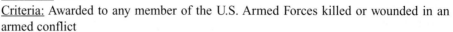

Silver   Bronze

Service: All Services (originally Army only)

Instituted: 1932

Criteria: Awarded to any member of the U.S. Armed Forces killed or wounded in an armed conflict

Devices: Army/Air Force: bronze, silver oak leaf cluster; Navy/ Marine Corps/Coast Guard: gold, silver star

Notes: Wound Ribbon appeared circa 1917-18 but was never officially authorized. (Army used wound chevrons during World War I)

     The Purple Heart is America's oldest military decoration. It was originally established on August 7, 1782 by General George Washington who designed the original medal, called the "Badge of Military Merit." The Badge of Military Merit was awarded for singularly meritorious action to a deserving hero of the Revolutionary War. There were only three recipients of the Badge of Military Merit; all three recipients were non-commissioned officers of the Continental Army. The Badge of Military Merit was intended by Washington to be a permanent decoration but was never used again after the three initial presentations until it was reestablished as the Purple Heart on February 22, 1932 by the Army War Department. General Douglas MacArthur, who was a key figure in its revival, received the first Purple Heart on July 21, 1932 after it was reestablished. President Franklin D. Roosevelt signed an executive order on December 3, 1942 that expanded authorization of the award to members of the Navy, Marine Corps, and Coast Guard as well. Although the Purple Heart was awarded for meritorious service between 1932 and 1943, the primary purpose of the award has always been to recognize those who received wounds while in the service of the United States military.

     President John F. Kennedy extended eligibility for the Purple Heart to civilians by an executive order signed on April 25, 1962. President Ronald R. Reagan, on February 23, 1984, authorized the Purple Heart for military and civilian personnel who received wounds from a terrorist attack or while performing peace keeping duties. Current criteria states that it is awarded for wounds received while serving in any capacity with one of the US Armed Forces after April 5, 1917; it may be awarded to civilians as well as military personnel. The wounds may have been received while in combat against an enemy, while a member of a peacekeeping force, while a Prisoner of War, as a result of a terrorist attack, or as a result of a friendly fire incident in hostile territory. The 1996 Defense Authorization Act extended eligibility for the Purple Heart to prisoners of war before April 25, 1962; previously, 1962 legislation had only authorized the medal to POWs after April 25, 1962. Wounds that qualify must have required treatment by a medical officer and must be a matter of official record.

     The Purple Heart was awarded to several hundred Air Force personnel who received wounds in the terrorist bombing attack upon an Air Force dormitory on June 25, 1996 in Dhahran, Saudi Arabia and to the family of the only Air Force officer killed in a friendly fire incident over Northern Iraq in 1994, First Lieutenant Laura A. Piper. The Purple Heart was originally behind all other decorations in precedence but was elevated to a position just behind the Bronze Star. The medal is a heart shaped purple gold-rimmed medallion with a profile of George Washington; above Washington's profile is the shield from his family's coat of arms. "FOR MILITARY MERIT" is inscribed on the reverse. The ribbon is a dark purple with narrow white edges. The color purple has historically represented sorrow and suffering while white represents comfort. The precedence of the Purple Heart was changed in 1984 to a position following the Bronze Star Medal; its previous position had been behind all other decorations for valor or meritorious service.

**1782 Badge of
Military Merit**

DEFENSE MERITORIOUS SERVICE MEDAL

Defense Meritorious Service Medal

Silver   Bronze

Service: All Services (by Secretary of Defense)
Instituted: 1977
Criteria: Noncombat meritorious achievement or service while assigned to the Joint Activity
Devices: Army/Air Force/ Navy/Marine Corps: bronze, silver oak leaf cluster; Coast Guard: gold, silver star
Notes: Coast Guard uses gold star device since the oak leaf cluster may not be worn on its uniform

Authorized on November 3, 1977. Awarded to any active member of the US Armed Forces who distinguishes him/herself by non-combat meritorious achievement or service while serving in a joint activity after November 3, 1977. Examples of Joint assignments that may allow qualification for this medal are: Office of the Secretary of Defense; Office of the Joint Chiefs of Staff; Unified or Specified Commands; Joint billets in NATO or NORAD; Defense Agencies; National Defense University, National War College, Industrial College of the Armed Forces and Armed Forces Staff College; and the Joint Strategic Target Planning Staff. Air Force Secretary Sheila Widnall awarded this medal posthumously to 1st LT. Laura A. Piper in recognition of her distinguished service and sacrifice to her country. Lt. Piper was the only Air Force casualty of the 1994 friendly fire shootdown of two U.S. Army helicopters by two Air Force jets over Northern Iraq that also killed 25 other military personnel. The bronze medal has an eagle with spread wings in the center superimposed on a pentagon in the center of a laurel wreath. The reverse is inscribed with the words "DEFENSE MERITORIOUS SERVICE" and "UNITED STATES OF AMERICA." Subsequent awards for Air Force personnel are denoted by oak leaf clusters.

MERITORIOUS SERVICE MEDAL

Meritorious Service Medal

Silver   Bronze

Service: All Services
Instituted: 1969
Criteria: Outstanding noncombat meritorious achievement or service to the United States
Devices: Army/Air Force: bronze, silver oak leaf cluster; Navy/ Marine Corps: gold, silver star; Coast Guard: silver letter "O", gold, silver star

Authorized on January 16, 1969 and awarded for non-combat meritorious achievement of meritorious service after that date to members of the Armed Forces. Additional awards are indicated for Air Force personnel by the attachment of bronze or silver oak leaf clusters. The Meritorious Service Medal evolved from an initial recommendation by the Commander, American Expeditionary Forces during World War I, General John J. Pershing in 1918; he suggested that an award for meritorious service be created to provide special recognition to deserving individuals by the U.S. government. Although the request by General Pershing was disapproved, it was revisited several more times during World War II and afterwards. During the Vietnam War the proposal to create the medal received significant attention and was eventually approved when President Lyndon B. Johnson signed the executive order on January 16, 1969. The Meritorious Service Medal cannot be awarded for service in a combat theater. It has often been the decoration of choice by the Air Force for both end of tour and retirement recognition for field grade officers and senior non-commissioned officers. The bronze medal depicts an eagle with outstretched wings standing on laurel branches in front of a large star; the reverse of the medal has the inscription "UNITED STATES OF AMERICA" at the top and "MERITORIOUS SERVICE" at the bottom.

AIR MEDAL

Silver   Bronze

<u>Service:</u> All Services
<u>Instituted:</u> 1942
<u>Criteria:</u> Heroic actions or meritorious service while participating in aerial flight
<u>Devices:</u> Army: bronze letter "V" (for valor), bronze numeral; Air Force: bronze, silver oak leaf cluster ; Navy/Marine Corps: bronze letter "V" (for valor), bronze numeral, gold numeral, bronze star , gold, silver star ; Coast Guard: gold, silver star

Authorized on May 11, 1942. Awarded for single acts of achievement after September 8, 1939 while participating in aerial flight to individuals who distinguish themselves by heroism, outstanding achievement, or by meritorious service. While there is no regulation that indicates so, it can be substantiated that many air medals were awarded after completion of a specified number of flights in combat areas in specific aircraft (for example, the author was awarded five air medals for completion of 100 combat missions in the B-52 during the Vietnam war — one air medal for each 20 missions). The act of achievement must be accomplished with distinction above and beyond that expected of professional airmen. While the Air Medal had been awarded for exceptional performance in peace time sustained flight operations, after January 1, 1990 the Aerial Achievement Medal provided this recognition and the Air Medal was awarded for specific acts of extraordinary achievement. The AAF and USAF have always used oak leaf clusters only to indicate additional awards while other services have used numerals. It is very common to see USAF personnel wearing two or more ribbons to properly show their number of awarded air medals since ribbons are allowed a maximum of five oak leaf attachments on each. It should also be noted that the Air Force does not authorize the V attachment on the Air Medal as do the other services. The medal is shaped as a compass rose and depicts a swooping American bald eagle with lightning bolts in its talons. The reverse of the compass rose is plain with an area for engraving of the recipient's name.

AERIAL ACHIEVEMENT MEDAL

Silver   Bronze

<u>Service:</u> Air Force
<u>Instituted:</u> 1988
<u>Criteria:</u> Sustained meritorious achievement while participating in aerial flight
<u>Devices:</u> Bronze, silver oak leaf cluster
<u>Notes:</u> Considered on a par with the Air Medal but more likely to be awarded for peacetime actions

Established on February 3, 1988 and effective since January 1, 1990. Awarded to USAF personnel for sustained meritorious achievement while participating in aerial flight. It is not awarded for single event flights; the missions and positions that may qualify for the award are identified by major command units. The American bald eagle is depicted on the front of the medal just below 13 stars symbolic of the original colonies and in front of two intercepting arcs symbolic of flight paths; the eagle is clutching six lightning bolts which represent the U.S. Air Force. The reverse contains the words "FOR MILITARY MERIT" surrounding a space for engraving of the awardee's name.

JOINT SERVICE COMMENDATION MEDAL

Joint Service Commendation Medal

V		
Bronze	Silver	Bronze

Service: All Services (by Secretary of Defense)
Instituted: 1963
Criteria: Meritorious service or achievement while assigned to a Joint Activity
Devices: Army/Air Force/ Navy/Marine Corps: bronze letter "V" (for valor), bronze, silver oak leaf cluster; Coast Guard: bronze letter "V" (for valor), gold, silver star
Notes: Coast Guard uses gold star device since the oak leaf cluster may not be worn on its uniform

Authorized on June 25, 1963, this was the first medal specifically authorized for members of a joint service organization. Awarded to members of the Armed Forces for meritorious achievement or service while serving in a joint activity after January 1, 1963. V device is authorized if the award is made for direct participation in combat operations. Oak leaf clusters denote additional awards. The medal consists of four conjoined hexagons of green enamel edged in gold with an eagle in the center that has 13 gold stars above it, all contained within a circular laurel wreath. Inscribed on the reverse of the medal are the words "FOR MILITARY" at the top and "MERIT" at the bottom.

AIR FORCE COMMENDATION MEDAL

Air Force Commendation Medal

V		
Bronze	Silver	Bronze

Service: Air Force
Instituted: 1958
Criteria: Outstanding achievement or meritorious service rendered on behalf of the United States Air Force
Devices: Bronze, silver oak leaf cluster, V attachment

Authorized on March 28, 1958; previous to this date the Army Commendation Medal was awarded to Air Force personnel who met the criteria for the award. Awarded to personnel below the rank of Brigadier General for outstanding achievement or meritorious service or acts of courage that do not meet the requirements for award of the Airman's Medal or the Bronze Star Medal. The medal has often been used for end of tour recognition, especially to junior officers and non-commissioned officers. In 1996, the Secretary of the Air Force authorized the award of a letter V for this medal if the award is given to Air Force members who distinguish themselves while under attack or during a hazardous situation resulting from hostilities — retroactive to January 11, 1996. The V may be awarded for actions taken during single acts of terrorism and isolated combat incidents. The first instances of the V device being awarded with this medal were for those awarded for actions during the terrorist bombing in Saudi Arabia in 1996. The front of the medal contains an American eagle with outstretched wings in front of a cloud formation and perched above the Air Force Coat of Arms. The reverse contains the words "FOR MILITARY MERIT."

ARMY COMMENDATION MEDAL

Bronze   Silver   Bronze

<u>Service:</u> Army
<u>Instituted:</u> 1945 (retroactive to 1941)
<u>Criteria:</u> Heroism, meritorious achievement or meritorious service
<u>Devices:</u> Bronze letter "V" (for valor), bronze, silver oak leaf cluster
<u>Notes:</u> Originally a ribbon-only award then designated "Army Commendation Ribbon with Metal Pendant". Redesignated: "Army Commendation Medal" in 1960

Authorized on December 18, 1945 as a commendation ribbon and awarded to members of the Armed Forces for heroism, meritorious achievement or meritorious service after December 6, 1941. It was the first Army decoration to be authorized only as a ribbon award. In 1962, it was authorized for award to a member of the Armed Forces of a friendly nation for the same level of achievement or service which was mutually beneficial to that nation and the United States. It was initially awarded for peacetime accomplishments but, later, in 1950 it was also authorized for appropriate achievements during combat. When the Air Force became a separate service in 1947, the ribbon was renamed the Commendation Ribbon to allow awarding to USAF personnel (the Air Force Commendation Medal was authorized in 1959). The metal pendant for the award was approved in 1949. A letter "V" device was authorized for this medal on February 29, 1964 for combat heroism of a degree less than that required for the Bronze Star Medal. The medal is a bronze hexagonal with the American bald eagle with spread wings on the face; the eagle has the U.S. shield on its breast and is grasping three crossed arrows. On the medal's reverse are the inscriptions "FOR MILITARY" and "MERIT."

JOINT SERVICE ACHIEVEMENT MEDAL

Silver   Bronze

<u>Service:</u> All Services (by Secretary of Defense)
<u>Instituted:</u> 1983
<u>Criteria:</u> Meritorious service or achievement while serving with a Joint Activity
<u>Devices:</u> Army/Air Force/ Navy/Marine Corps: bronze, silver oak leaf cluster
Coast Guard: gold, silver star
<u>Notes:</u> Coast Guard uses gold star device since the oak leaf cluster may not be worn on its uniform

Awarded for meritorious service or achievement while serving in a joint activity after August 3, 1983 to members below the rank of colonel (or Navy captain). Oak leaf clusters denote additional awards for Air Force personnel. An American eagle with the United States coat of arms on its breast adorns the center of the bronze medal which consists of a star of twelve points. The reverse of the medal contains the inscriptions "JOINT SERVICE" and "ACHIEVEMENT AWARD."

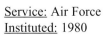

AIR FORCE ACHIEVEMENT MEDAL

Air Force Achievement Medal

Bronze   Silver   Bronze

Service: Air Force
Instituted: 1980
Criteria: Outstanding achievement or meritorious service not warranting award of the Air Force Commendation Medal
Devices: Bronze, silver oak leaf cluster, V attachment

The Air Force Achievement Medal was established by the Secretary of the Air Force on October 12, 1980 and may be awarded to US military personnel below the rank of colonel for meritorious service or outstanding achievement. This medal is the first decoration established for Air Force personnel under Air Force authority. The primary use of the medal has been to recognize specific individual achievements or accomplishments rather than continuing periods of service such as might be associated with a change in permanent assignment, although it has been used for end of tour recognition for some junior ranking personnel. A letter V was authorized retroactive to January 11, 1996 for those receiving the award for actions during combat conditions, hostile acts, or single acts of terrorism; the first instances of the "V" device being awarded with the medal were to airmen who received the medal for actions during the 1996 terrorist bombing of an Air Force dormitory in Saudi Arabia. The front of the medal has eleven cog-like shapes on the outer border; within the medal are a set of wings with four thunderbolts crossing through them. The reverse of the medal bears the circular inscription, "AIR FORCE MERITORIOUS ACHIEVEMENT."

ARMY/AIR FORCE PRESIDENTIAL UNIT CITATION

Air Force Presidential Unit Citation

Silver   Bronze

Service: Air Force
Instituted: 1957
Criteria: Awarded to Air Force units for extraordinary heroism in action against an armed enemy
Devices: Bronze, silver oak leaf cluster
Notes: Original designation: Distinguished Unit Citation. Redesignated to present name in 1957

Established on February 26, 1942 as the "Distinguished Unit Badge" or the "Distinguished Unit Citation" during World War II, the award was redesignated as the Presidential Unit Citation on January 10, 1957. This award is a ribbon award only and was worn on the right chest of AAF personnel during WWII. It is awarded to Army and Air Force units that display the same degree of heroism in combat as would warrant the Distinguished Service Cross for an individual. The gold frame around the ribbon was a larger size for AAF personnel than the one used by USAF personnel which is worn with other ribbons on the left chest. The gold-colored frame around the ribbon is worn with the open end of the "V" pattern pointing upward. Awarded to members of the cited organization; may be worn permanently by members assigned to the unit for the period for which it was awarded. Members of the unit who were not assigned to the unit for the award period may only wear the ribbon while assigned to the unit.

JOINT MERITORIOUS UNIT AWARD

Silver   Bronze

Service: All Services
Instituted: 1982
Criteria: Awarded to Joint Service units for meritorious achievement
or service in combat or extreme circumstances
Devices: Army/Air Force/ Navy/Marine Corps: bronze, silver oak
leaf cluster; Coast Guard: bronze, silver star

　　　Authorized on June 10, 1981 and awarded to joint units and activities for meritorious achievement or service, superior to that which is normally expected, during action in combat, in a declared national emergency situation, or under extraordinary circumstances that involve national interests. Only those members of the U.S. Armed Forces who were present at the time and directly participated in the service or achievement for 30 days (less if the operation was for a period less than 30 days) are authorized to wear the ribbon award. Members must be assigned and/or attached by official orders to the joint unit receiving the ribbon, either as individuals or as members of an assigned or attached unit. The award is retroactive to 23 January 1979. The ribbon is worn within a gold-colored frame with the open end of the "V" pattern pointing upward.

AIR FORCE OUTSTANDING UNIT AWARD (AFOUA)

Outstanding Unit Award

Bronze   Silver   Bronze

Service: Air Force
Instituted: 1954
Criteria: Awarded to U.S. Air Force units for exceptionally meri-
torious achievement or meritorious service
Devices: Bronze letter "V", bronze, silver oak leaf cluster

　　　Established on January 6, 1954. Awarded by the Secretary of the Air Force to units for exceptionally meritorious service or outstanding achievement that clearly sets the unit above and apart from similar units. A unit must clearly perform at a high level for a sustained period of time to receive such recognition as afforded by this award. A bronze letter V is worn on the ribbon when awarded for combat or direct combat support actions; this valor designation is listed in Air Force regulations that list unit awards and combat designations. The exceptionally meritorious service must have been performed for a period of not more than two years and not less than one year.

 **AIR FORCE ORGANIZATIONAL EXCELLENCE AWARD (AFOEA)**

Organizational Excellence Award

Bronze   Silver   Bronze

Service: Air Force
Instituted: 1969
Criteria: Same as Outstanding Unit Award but awarded to unique unnumbered organizations performing staff functions
Devices: Bronze letter "V", bronze, silver oak leaf cluster

Established on August 26, 1969. The award recognizes units that have performed exceptionally meritorious service for a nominated time period. It is awarded to recognize the achievements and accomplishments of Air Force organizations or activities that do not meet the eligibility requirements of the AFOUA. Two recent examples of units receiving the award are Headquarters U.S. Air Forces in Europe for the period July 1, 1994 to June 30, 1996 and Headquarters Air Force Academy who earned its fourth award for the period from September 1, 1994 to August 31, 1996. The letter V is authorized if awarded for combat or direct combat support actions. Recommendations for this award must cover a period of not less than 2 years. Normally, individual personnel records are automatically updated to show the award.

 **PRISONER OF WAR MEDAL**

Prisoner of War Medal

Silver   Bronze

Service: All Services
Instituted: 1986
Criteria: Awarded to any member of the U.S. Armed Forces taken prisoner during any armed conflict dating from World War I
Devices: Bronze, silver star

Authorized on November 8, 1985 and signed into law by President Ronald Reagan in 1986 for any person, who, while serving in any capacity with the U.S. Armed Forces, was taken prisoner and held captive after April 5, 1917. Relatives of Missing in Action (MIA) may receive the medal only if the military personnel or civilian had received credit for military service and their status as prisoners of war has been officially confirmed by the Military Departments and Department of Defense. The medal is issued only to those taken prisoner by an enemy during armed conflicts; hostages of terrorists and other governments with which the United States is not engaged in armed conflict are not eligible for the medal. World War II Merchant Marines and civilians who have been credited with military service, which includes a period of captivity, are also eligible for the medal. Bronze stars are authorized for additional awards. Escapees who do not return to U.S. military control and are subsequently recaptured by an enemy do not qualify for a subsequent award of the medal. It would obviously be unlikely to see someone who in fact qualified for attachments to the POW medal; however, Colonel Vernon P. Ligon, Jr., an AAF and USAF pilot who served and was captured in World War II, the Korean War, and the Vietnam War, was certainly eligible to wear the medal with two bronze stars signifying his POW status in all three wars. The front of the circular bronze medal has the American eagle, with wings folded, surrounded by barbed wire and bayonet points; the reverse of the medal has the U.S. shield and the inscriptions "AWARDED TO" and "FOR HONORABLE SERVICE WHILE A PRISONER OF WAR" and the words "UNITED STATES OF AMERICA" on the lower outer edge.

MERITORIOUS UNIT COMMENDATION

Silver   Bronze

Service: Army
Instituted: 1944
Criteria: Awarded to U.S. Army units for exceptionally meritorious conduct in the performance of outstanding service
Devices: Bronze, silver oak leaf cluster
Notes: Originally a golden wreath worn on the lower sleeve. Authorized in its present form in 1961

Awarded to units for exceptionally meritorious conduct in performance of outstanding services for at least 6 continuous months during the period of military operations against an armed enemy occurring on or after January 1, 1944. Service in a combat zone is not required but must be directly related to the combat effort. Units based within the continental U.S. or outside the area of operation are excluded from this award. The unit must display such outstanding devotion and superior performance of exceptional difficult tasks as to set it apart and above other units with similar missions. The award could be made to units for services performed during World War II only during the time period between January 1, 1944 and September 15, 1946. The award was usually given to units larger than battalions. The degree of achievement required is the same as that which would warrant award of the Legion of Merit to an individual. It was originally authorized as a wreath emblem that was worn on the lower right sleeve of the Army (AAF) uniform. As with other unit citations, it has a gold frame surrounding the ribbon; the open end of the "V" shaped design on the frame points upward. Army Air Force personnel wore this ribbon with other unit citations on the right side of the uniform separate from other ribbons worn on the left side of the uniform. Those AAF personnel who transitioned into the USAF in 1947 would wear the ribbon award on the left side of the uniform with all other ribbons. The gold frame is smaller when the ribbon is worn on the USAF uniform with other awards. Authorization for the award is contained in Army regulations that cited units and award periods.

COMBAT READINESS MEDAL

Combat Readiness Medal

Silver   Bronze

Service: Air Force
Instituted: 1964
Criteria: Awarded for specific periods of qualifying service in a combat or mission-ready status
Devices: Bronze, silver oak leaf cluster

Authorized on March 9, 1964. Awarded for periods of qualifying service in a combat or mission ready status for direct weapon system employment. Direct weapon system employment is defined as: (1) An aircrew whose wartime mission places them into enemy territory or in the threat envelope of ground enemy defenses; (2) A missile operation which could employ weapons to destroy enemy targets; and (3) Individuals who directly control inflight manned aircraft whose wartime mission is to seek and destroy enemy targets. An individual must be a member of a unit subject to combat readiness reporting under Joint Chiefs of Staff requirements, must have completed all prerequisite training and be certified as combat or mission ready in performing the unit's mission, and must be subject to a continuous individual positional evaluation program. In previous regulations, eligibility was extended to Air Force members on special duty with another U.S. military service provided they were certified as combat ready in that service and the combat ready status closely correlated to that of the Air Force. Originally an individual was required to be combat ready for three years to earn this award; currently, individuals must have 24 months of sustained combat ready status to receive the award. Eligibility for the award is certified by the individuals unit commander and is filed in the unit's personnel records group. An oak leaf cluster attachment is awarded for each additional 24 months of combat ready status provided there is no break greater than 120 days. The front of the medal has a border of concentric rays encircling a ring of stylized cloud forms with two intersecting triangles on a compass rose that has small triangles at his points. The reverse of the medal contains the inscription, "FOR COMBAT READINESS-AIR FORCE."

AIR FORCE GOOD CONDUCT MEDAL

Air Force Good Conduct Medal

Silver   Bronze

Service: Air Force
Instituted: 1963
Criteria: Exemplary conduct, efficiency and fidelity during three years of active enlisted service with the U.S. Air Force
Devices: Bronze, silver oak leaf cluster

Authorized on June 1, 1963. Awarded to Air Force personnel in an enlisted status upon recommendation of the unit commander for exemplary conduct while in active military service on or after June 1, 1963 after 3 years of continuous service (1 year in wartime- this was rarely done). The U. S. Air Force used the Army Good Conduct Medal to recognize deserving service by enlisted personnel from 1947 to 1963, when a medal was created specifically for the USAF. As with the Army Good Conduct Medal, the award was never automatic and required commander certification prior to being awarded. Commanders would usually receive notification from their personnel center that an individual was eligible for this award; the commander would then review the individuals record and would affix his/her signature to the personnel document verifying that the person was eligible and deserving of the award. The absence of an award of the Air Force Good Conduct medal to personnel who had a qualifying period of enlistment would be noteworthy to supervisory personnel. Bronze and silver oak leaf attachments are authorized to denote additional awards of the medal. The front of the medal bears the inscription, "EFFICIENCY, HONOR, FIDELITY," surrounding the American eagle which stands on a closed book and sword. On the reverse is a five-pointed star above a blank scroll; the words, "FOR GOOD," are above the star and below the scroll is the word,"CONDUCT."

ARMY GOOD CONDUCT MEDAL

Army Good Conduct Medal

Gold, Silver or Bronze Clasp

Service: Army
Instituted: 1941
Criteria: Exemplary conduct, efficiency and fidelity during three years of active enlisted service with the U.S. Army (1 year during wartime)
Devices: Bronze, silver, gold knotted bar

Authorized on June 28, 1941 to Army and AAF personnel for exemplary conduct, efficiency, and fidelity who on or after August 27, 1940 had honorably completed three years of active Federal military service. The award could also be awarded for one year of service after December 7, 1941 while the U.S. was at war; it should be noted that the award could be for a period as little as one year in wartime but was rarely given for that period of time. The award was not automatic and required certification by a commanding authority. It was awarded to USAF personnel until June 1, 1963 when the USAF Good Conduct Medal was instituted. Medal design is the same as the Air Force Good Conduct Medal. A bronze, silver, or gold clasp with knots (or loops) is attached to the medal/ribbon to indicate total number of awards. Unlike other awards, the number of knots does not mean additional awards but rather the total number of awards; for instance, two awards of the Army Good Conduct Medal are indicated by two bronze knots, three by three, etc. Six total awards are indicated by one silver knot, seven by two silver knots, etc. Eleven total awards are indicated by one gold knot, twelve by two gold knots, etc. While current regulations and regulations of World War II only authorize a clasp to represent a second award or higher; it is not unusual to see veterans with a single bronze knot on their good conduct medal or ribbon; this may have indicated either a single or second award and seems to have been an accepted practice.

AIR RESERVE FORCES MERITORIOUS SERVICE MEDAL

Air Reserve Forces Meritorious Service Medal

Silver   Bronze

Service: Air Force
Instituted: 1964
Criteria: Exemplary behavior, efficiency and fidelity during three years of active enlisted service with the Air Force Reserve
Devices: Bronze, silver oak leaf cluster

Authorized on April 1, 1964 as a ribbon award only; the medal was created in 1973. Awarded on specific recommendation of the unit commander to enlisted members of the Air Reserve Forces for exemplary behavior, efficiency, and fidelity for a period of 4 continuous years service prior to July 1, 1972 and for 3 years on/after July 1, 1972. Creditable service ends when called to active duty. The front of the medal has the American eagle perched atop a small circle containing a five-pointed star; a banner sits above the eagle and contains the words, "MERITORIOUS SERVICE." On the outer edge of the medal are the words, "AIR RESERVE FORCES." On the reverse is a cloud design with thunderbolts and wings with the word, "TO" inscribed below it and "EXEMPLARY BEHAVIOR-EFFICIENCY-FIDELITY" inscribed along the circular outer edge.

OUTSTANDING AIRMAN OF THE YEAR RIBBON

Outstanding Airman of the Year Ribbon

Bronze   Silver Bronze

Service: Air Force
Instituted: 1968
Criteria: Awarded to airmen for selection to the "12 Outstanding Airmen of the Year" Competition Program
Devices: Bronze, silver oak leaf cluster, bronze star

Authorized on February 21, 1968. Awarded to those 12 airmen chosen from nominees throughout the Air Force, field operation agencies, the Air Force Reserve and Air National Guard in the 12 Outstanding Airmen of the Year Program. The ribbon is retroactive to include those selected for this program as of June 1970. The 12 current designees wear a bronze service star and multiple winners wear oak leaf clusters to denote additional awards.

AIR FORCE RECOGNITION RIBBON

Air Force Recognition Ribbon

Silver   Bronze

Service: Air Force
Instituted: 1980
Criteria: Awarded to individual recipients of Air Force-level special trophies and awards
Devices: Bronze, silver oak leaf cluster

Authorized on October 12, 1980 and effective January 1, 1981. Awarded to individual recipients of Air Force level special trophies and awards, as listed in appropriate Air Force regulations, except the 12 Outstanding Airmen of the Year nominees. It is not awarded to individuals of a unit when the unit receives a special award. The ribbon is not awarded retroactively. Oak leaf clusters denote additional awards.

AMERICAN DEFENSE SERVICE MEDAL

Bronze

Service: All Services
Instituted: 1941
Dates: 1939-41
Criteria: Army: 12 months of active duty service during the above period; Naval Services: Any active duty service
Devices: All Services: bronze star (denotes bars below); All Naval Services: bronze letter "A" (not worn with bronze star above)
Bars: Army/Air Force: "Foreign Service", All Naval Services: "Base", "Fleet", Coast Guard: "Sea"

Authorized on June 28, 1941 for military service during the limited emergency proclaimed by President Roosevelt on Sept. 8, 1939 or during the unlimited emergency proclaimed on May 27, 1941 until December 7, 1941 if under orders to active duty for 12 months or longer. The only attachment authorized for Army personnel during that period was the Foreign Service clasp (for medal only) if service was outside of the continental U.S.; to denote entitlement to a service clasp, a bronze star is worn on the service ribbon. The Navy and Marine Corps each had two clasps, the Fleet clasp for service on vessels of the fleet during the period, and the Base clasp for service on shore at bases and naval stations outside the continental U.S. The Coast Guard awarded a SEA clasp for personnel at sea during the period. On the front of the medal is the Grecian figure, Columbia, representing America or Liberty, holding a shield and sword while standing on an oak branch, symbolic of strength. The oak leaves represent the strength of the Army, Navy, Marine Corps, and Coast Guard. The inscription, "American Defense," is around the outside upper edge. The reverse of the medal carries the inscription "For Service During the Limited Emergency Proclaimed By the President on September 8, 1939 or During the Unlimited Emergency Proclaimed By the President on May 27, 1941." The golden yellow color of the ribbon symbolizes the golden opportunity of United States youth to serve the nation, represented by the blue, white, and red stripes on both sides of the ribbon.

WOMEN'S ARMY CORPS SERVICE MEDAL

Service: Army
Instituted: 1943
Dates: 1941-46
Criteria: Service with both the Women's Army Auxiliary Corps and Women's Army Corps during the above period
Devices: None
Notes: Only U.S. award authorized for women only.

Authorized on July 29, 1943 for service in both the Women's Army Auxiliary Corps (WAAC) between July 10, 1942 and August 31, 1943 and the Women's Army Corps (WAC) between September 1, 1943 and September 2, 1945. After 1945, members of the WAC received the same medals as other members of the Army. No attachments are authorized for the medal. The front of the medal contains the head of Pallas Athena, goddess of victory and wisdom, superimposed on a sword crossed with oak leaves and a palm branch. The sword represents military might; the oak leaves represent strength and the palm branch represents peace. The reverse contains thirteen stars, an eagle, and a scroll along with the words, "FOR SERVICE IN THE WOMEN'S AUXILIARY CORPS," and the dates "1942-1943." The dates on the medal, 1942-1943, remained the same even after the WAAC became the WAC. The ribbon is moss green with old gold edges, the branch colors of the Women's Army Corps. Green indicates merit and gold refers to achievement. Less than 100,000 women in World War II qualified for the Women's Army Corps Service Medal; over 40,000 WAC were assigned to the U.S. Army Air Force by 1945. This is the only service medal specifically created and authorized for women in the military.

AMERICAN CAMPAIGN MEDAL

American Campaign Medal

Bronze

Service: All Services
Instituted: 1942
Dates: 1941-46
Criteria: Service outside the U.S. in the American theater for 30 days, or within the continental U.S. for one year.
Devices: All Services: bronze, silver star; Navy: bronze Marine Corps device; Navy/Marine Corps: silver star (obsolete)

Authorized on November 6, 1942, as amended on March 15, 1946. Awarded for service within the American Theater between December 7, 1941 and March 2, 1946. Qualifications for this medal include an aggregate service of one year within the continental US(CONUS), permanent assignment outside the CONUS for at least 30 consecutive or 60 non-consecutive days between December 7, 1941 and March 2, 1946, or active combat against the enemy during the prescribed period. While Army regulations list three campaigns, all with the same dates noted previously (Antisubmarine, Ground Combat, and Air Combat), there was, in fact, only one campaign that involved combat operations, the Antisubmarine Campaign. Those individuals serving with a unit that was awarded battle credit for the Antisubmarine Campaign in the American Theater, received a bronze service star for wear on the American Campaign Medal drape and ribbon bar. After the attack on Pearl Harbor, the United States Army Air Force was assigned responsibility for aerial antisubmarine warfare over U.S. coastal waters off of both coasts, in the Caribbean Sea, the Gulf of Mexico, the Atlantic Ocean near Newfoundland, and the waters on both sides of the Panama Canal. Qualifying duties included escort duties for naval vessels, involving both ships and aircraft, and active air/sea operations against enemy submarines operating in American Theater waters. The Second and Fourth Air Forces began patrols off of the west coast on December 8, 1941 using medium bombers. The I Bomber Command began patrols off of the east coast also on December 8, 1941. In October 1942, when Germany began focusing its submarine operations in the North Atlantic, the Army Air Forces Antisubmarine Command (AAFAC) was created and placed under operational control of the U.S. Navy. In 1943, sole responsibility for antisubmarine operations on the west coast was given to the Fourth Air Force. The AAFAC was inactivated on August 31, 1943 and complete responsibility for antisubmarine operations was given to the Navy. While no submarines were sunk off of the west coast during the war, the AAF did successfully attack many enemy submarines off of the east coast. It should be noted that the American Theater included both North and South America but did not cover Alaska, Hawaii, and Greenland. The front of the medal shows a B-24 aircraft flying above a Navy cruiser and a sinking submarine above three waves in the foreground. The buildings in the background represent the arsenal of democracy. The reverse is identical to the Asiatic-Pacific and European-African-Middle Eastern Campaign Medals and portrays the American eagle, symbol of power, perched on a rock, the symbol of stability, and the inscriptions, "1941-1945" and "UNITED STATES OF AMERICA." The main color of the ribbon, azure blue, stands for the Americas while the central blue, white, and red thin stripes refer to the continued defense of the Americas after Pearl Harbor. The black and white stripes of the ribbon represent Germany while the red and white stripes represent Japan. When wearing the ribbon bar, wear it with the blue stripe in the center of the ribbon to the wearer's right and the red stripe to the wearer's left.

Designated campaign for the American Campaign Medal is:

1. Antisubmarine Campaign -- December 7, 1941 - September 2, 1945

EUROPEAN-AFRICAN-MIDDLE EASTERN CAMPAIGN MEDAL

European-African-Middle Eastern Campaign

Bronze   Silver   Bronze

Service: All Services
Instituted: 1942
Dates: 1941-45
Criteria: Service in the European-African-Middle Eastern theater for 30 days or receipt of any combat decoration
Devices: All Services: bronze, silver star; Army/Air Force: bronze arrowhead; Navy: bronze Marine Corps device; Navy/Marine Corps: silver star (obsolete)

Authorized on November 6, 1942, as amended on March 15, 1946. Awarded to members of the U.S. Armed Forces for at least 30 days of consecutive (60 days non-consecutive) service within the European Theater of Operations between December 7, 1941 and November 8, 1945 (lesser periods qualify if individual was in actual combat against the enemy during this period). A bronze star attachment is authorized for participation in one of the 17 designated campaigns in the European Theater; a silver star attachment should be used in lieu of five bronze stars to indicate five campaigns. Each of the designated campaigns had a designated combat zone and specific dates. Campaign credits were not authorized for those personnel or units serving after the date of Germany's unconditional surrender, May 11, 1945. An arrowhead attachment is authorized for participation in a combat parachute jump, combat glider landing, or amphibious assault landing; although many individuals qualified for more than one arrowhead, only one arrowhead attachment is authorized for each medal/ribbon. The front of the bronze medal shows a Landing Ship Tank unloading troops while under fire with an airplane overhead. The reverse has the American eagle, symbol of power, standing on a rock, symbol of stability, with the inscription "UNITED STATES OF AMERICA" and dates "1941-1945." The ribbon's central blue, white, and red stripes represent the United States. The wide green stripes represent the green fields of Europe; the brown stripes on each edge represent the African desert sands; the green, white, and red thin stripes represent Italy; and the black and white thin stripes represent Germany.

Designated campaigns for the European-African-Middle Eastern Campaign Medal are:

1. Air Combat -- December 7, 1941 - September 2, 1945
2. Egypt-Libya -- June 11, 1942 - February 12, 1943
3. Algeria-French Morocco -- November 8-11, 1942
4. Tunisia -- November 12, 1942 - May 13, 1943
5. Sicily -- May 14 - August 17, 1943
6. Naple-Foggia -- August 18, 1943 - January 21, 1944
7. Anzio -- January 22 - May 24, 1944
8. Rome-Arno -- January 22 - September 9, 1944
9. North Apennines -- September 10, 1944 - April 4, 1945
10. Po Valley -- April 5 - May 8, 1945
11. Air Offensive, Europe -- July 4, 1942 - June 5, 1944
12. Normandy -- June 6 - July 24, 1944
13. Northern France -- July 25 - September 14, 1944
14. Southern France -- August 15 - September 14, 1944
15. Rhineland -- September 15, 1944 - March 21, 1945
16. Ardennes-Alsace -- December 16, 1944 - January 25, 1945
17. Central Europe -- March 22 - May 11, 1945

ASIATIC-PACIFIC CAMPAIGN MEDAL

Asiatic-Pacific Campaign Medal

Bronze   Silver   Bronze

Service: All Services
Instituted: 1942
Dates: 1941-46
Criteria: Service in the Asiatic-Pacific theater for 30 day or receipt of any combat decoration
Devices: All Services: bronze, silver star; Army/Air Force: bronze arrowhead; Navy: bronze Marine Corps device; Navy/Marine Corps: silver star (obsolete)

Authorized on November 6, 1942, and amended on March 15, 1946. Awarded to members of the U.S. Armed Forces for at least 30 consecutive (60 non-consecutive) days service (less if in combat) within the Asiatic-Pacific Theater between December 7, 1941 and March 2, 1946. There were 21 campaigns designated by area and dates in the Pacific Theater; campaign credit was not awarded to personnel or units who served in the theater after Japan formally surrendered on September 2, 1945. A bronze star is authorized for attachment to the ribbon and medal for participation in a campaign. A silver star attachment is used to represent five bronze stars or involvement in five different campaigns. An arrowhead attachment is authorized for participation in a combat parachute jump, combat glider landing, or amphibious assault landing (only one arrowhead may be worn on the medal/ribbon despite the number of qualification events). The front of the medal shows a palm tree amidst troops with an aircraft overhead and an aircraft carrier, battleship, and submarine in the background. The reverse has the American eagle, symbolizing power, on a rock, symbolizing stability, with the inscription "UNITED STATES OF AMERICA" on the eagle's back. The orange yellow of the ribbon represents Asia while the white-red stripes toward each edge represent Japan. The center blue, white, and red thin stripes are taken from the American Defense Service Medal, referring to America's continued defense preparedness after Pearl Harbor. The ribbon is worn with the center blue stripe on the wearer's right.

Designated campaigns for the Asiatic-Pacific Campaign Medal are:

1. Central Pacific -- December 7, 1941 - December 6, 1943
2. Philippine Islands -- December 7, 1941 - May 10, 1942
3. East Indies -- January 1 - July 22, 1942
4. Papua -- July 23, 1942 - January 23, 1943
5. Aleutian Islands -- June 3, 1942 - August 24, 1943
6. Guadalcanal -- August 7, 1942 - February 21, 1943
7. Northern Solomons -- February 22, 1943 - November 21, 1944
8. Bismarck Archipelago -- December 15, 1943 - November 27, 1944
9. Eastern Mandates -- December 7, 1943 - April 16, 1944
10. Western Pacific -- April 17, 1944 - September 2, 1945
11. New Guinea -- January 24, 1943 - December 31, 1944
12. Leyte -- October 17, 1944 - July 1, 1945
13. Luzon -- December 15, 1944 - July 4, 1945
14. Southern Philippines -- February 27 - July 4, 1945
15. Burma -- December 7, 1941 - May 26, 1942
16. India-Burma -- April 2, 1942 - January 28, 1945
17. Central Burma -- January 29 - July 15, 1945
18. China Defensive -- July 4, 1942 - May 4, 1945
19. China Offensive -- May 5 - September 2, 1945
20. Ryukus -- March 26 - July 2, 1945
21. Air Offensive, Japan -- April 17, 1942 - September 2, 1945

WORLD WAR II VICTORY MEDAL

World War II Victory Medal

None

Service: All Services
Instituted: 1945
Dates: 1941-46
Criteria: Awarded for service in the U.S. Armed Forces during the above period
Devices: None

Authorized by Congress on July 6, 1945 and awarded to members of the Armed Forces for service between December 7, 1941 and December 31, 1946, inclusive. No attachments are authorized although some veterans received the medal with an affixed bronze star which according to them was to distinguish those who served in combat from those who didn't (I've not found any documentation to support this). Many World War II veterans do not have this medal on their separation documents since many were discharged prior to the medal being authorized. The front of the medal depicts the Liberty figure resting her right foot on a war god's helmet with the hilt of a broken sword in her right hand and the broken blade in her left hand. The reverse contains the words, "FREEDOM FROM FEAR AND WANT," "FREEDOM OF SPEECH AND RELIGION," and "UNITED STATES OF AMERICA 1941-1945." The red center stripe of the ribbon is symbolic of Mars, God of War, representing both courage and fortitude. The twin rainbow stripes, suggested by the World War I Victory Medal, allude to the peace following a storm. A narrow white stripe separates the center red stripe from each rainbow pattern on both sides of the ribbon. The World War II Victory Medal provides deserving recognition to all of America's veterans who served during World War II.

ARMY OF OCCUPATION MEDAL

Army of Occupation Medal

 Gold Airplane

Service: Army/Air Force
Instituted: 1946
Dates: 1945-55 (Berlin: 1945-90)
Criteria: 30 consecutive days of service in occupied territories of former enemies during above period
Devices: Gold airplane
Bars: "Germany", "Japan"

Authorized on June 7, 1946 and awarded to both Army, Army Air Force, and USAF personnel for at least 30 consecutive days of service in formerly held enemy territory-- includes Germany (1945-1955), Berlin (1945-1990), Austria (1945-1955), Italy (1945-1947), Japan (1945-1952), and Korea (1945-1949). A gold colored C-54 airplane device is authorized to denote participation in the Berlin airlift. Germany and Japan clasp attachments are authorized for the medal only (no attachment authorized for ribbon) for occupation service in those respective territories; an individual who performed occupational service in both areas is authorized to wear both clasp attachments on the drape of the medal with the upper clasp representing the area where occupation was first performed. The front of the medal depicts the Remagen Bridge on the Rhine River and the reverse depicts Mount Fujiyama in Japan with two Japanese junks in front of the mountain. Although not specifically authorized by regulations many veterans received their Occupation Medals with reversed medallions in order to show the theater of occupation service (i.e. if occupation service was in Japan, the side with Mount Fujiyama was the front of the medal). The white and black colors of the ribbon represent Germany and the white and red colors represent Japan.

MEDAL FOR HUMANE ACTION

Service: All Services
Instituted: 1949
Dates: 1948-49
Criteria: 120 consecutive days of service participating in the Berlin Airlift or in support thereof
Devices: None

Authorized for members of the U.S. Armed Forces on July 20, 1949 for at least 120 days of service while participating in or providing direct support for the Berlin Airlift during the period June 26, 1948 and September 30, 1949. The prescribed boundaries for qualifying service include the area between the north latitudes of the 54th and the 48th parallels and between the 14th east longitude and the 5th west longitude meridians. No attachments are authorized. A common mistake is to put the C-54 airplane attachment on this medal instead of on the correct medal, the Occupation Medal. Posthumous award may be made to any person who lost his/her life while, or as a direct result of, participating in the Berlin airlift, without regard to the length of such service. The front of the medal depicts the C-54 aircraft ,which did the majority of the airlift, above the coat of arms of Berlin which lies in the center of a wreath of wheat. The reverse has the American eagle with shield and arrows and bears the inscriptions, "FOR HUMANE ACTION" and "TO SUPPLY NECESSITIES OF LIFE TO THE PEOPLE OF BERLIN GERMANY."

NATIONAL DEFENSE SERVICE MEDAL

Service: All Services
Instituted: 1953
Dates: 1950-54, 1961-74, 1990-95
Criteria: Any honorable active duty service during any of the above periods
Devices: All Services: bronze star ; Army: bronze oak leaf cluster (obsolete)
Notes: Reinstituted in 1966 and 1991 for Vietnam and Southwest Asia (Gulf War) actions respectively

Initially authorized by executive order on April 22, 1953. Awarded to members of the U.S. Armed Forces for any honorable active federal service during the Korean War (June 27, 1950-July 27, 1954), Vietnam War (January 1, 1961-August 14, 1974), and Desert Shield/Desert Storm (August 2, 1990-November 30, 1995). Today, there are probably more people authorized this medal than any other medal. It is often referred to in terms such as "the alive in 65" medal and the "I was in" medal. While many people did receive this medal, there were many who served outside of those eligibility periods and did not receive any medal for service. Circumstances not qualifying as active duty for the purpose of this medal include: (1) Members of the Guard and Reserve on short tours of active duty to fulfill training obligations; (2) Service members on active duty to serve on boards, courts, commissions, and like organizations; (3) Service members on active duty for the sole purpose of undergoing a physical examination; and (4) Service members on active duty for purposes other than extended active duty. Reserve personnel who have received the Armed Forces Expeditionary Medal or the Vietnam Service Medal are eligibile for this medal. The National Defense Service Medal is also authorized to those individuals serving as cadets or midshipmen at the Air Force, Army, or Naval Academies. No more than one medal is awarded to a single individual. Bronze star attachments have always been the only authorized attachments for additional awards for USAF personnel. The front of the medal has the American bald eagle with inverted wings standing on a sword and palm branch and contains the words "NATIONAL DEFENSE"; the reverse has the United States shield amidst an oak leaf and laurel spray.

KOREAN SERVICE MEDAL

Korean Service Medal

Bronze   Silver   Bronze

Service: All Services
Instituted: 1950
Dates: 1950-54
Criteria: Participation in military operations within the Korean area during the above period
Devices: All Services: bronze, silver star ; Army/Air Force: bronze arrowhead; Navy: bronze Marine Corps device

Authorized by executive order on November 8, 1950 and awarded for service between June 27, 1950 and July 27, 1954 in the Korean theater of operations. Members of the U.S. Armed Forces must have participated in combat or served with a combat or service unit in the Korean Theater for 30 consecutive or 60 non-consecutive days during the designated period. Personnel who served with a unit or headquarters stationed outside the theater but directly supported Korean military operations are also entitled to this medal. The combat zone designated for qualification for the medal encompassed both North and South Korea, Korean waters, and the airspace over these areas. Bronze/silver star attachments are authorized to be affixed to the suspension drape and ribbon bar to indicate participation in any or all of the 10 designated campaigns in the Korean War. The first campaign began when North Korea first invaded South Korea and the last campaign ended when the Korean Armistice cease-fire became effective. The Far East Air Force (FEAF) Bomber Command and the Fifth Air Force provided air interdiction, close air support, and reconnaissance while punishing the enemy with major attacks on its transportation networks, industrial targets, and even its capital city of Pyongyang. Army personnel who participated in an amphibious assault landing are entitled to wear an arrowhead attachment on the ribbon and medal. A Korean gateway is depicted on the front of the medal along with the inscription "KOREAN SERVICE" and on the reverse is a Korean symbol from the Korean flag that represents unity and the inscription "UNITED STATES OF AMERICA." A spray of oak and laurel line the bottom edge. The suspension ribbon and ribbon bar are both blue, representing the United Nations, with a narrow, white stripe on each edge and a white band in the center. The period of Korean service was extended by one year from the cease fire by the Secretary of Defense; individuals could qualify for the medal during this period if stationed in Korea but would not receive any campaign credit. An award of this medal qualified personnel for award of the United Nations (Korean) Service Medal also.

Designated campaigns for the Korea Service Medal are:

1. UN Defensive -- June 27 - September 15, 1950
2. UN Offensive -- September 16 - November 2, 1950
3. CCF Intervention -- November 3, 1950 - January 24, 1951
4. 1st UN Counteroffensive -- January 25 - April 21, 1951
5. CCF Spring Offensive -- April 22 - July 8, 1951
6. UN Summer-Fall Offensive -- July 9 - November 27, 1951
7. Second Korean Winter -- November 28, 1951 - April 30, 1952
8. Korea, Summer-Fall -- May 1 - November 30, 1953
9. Third Korean Winter -- December 1, 1952 - April 30, 1953
10. Korea, Summer -- May 1 - July 27, 1953

ANTARCTICA SERVICE MEDAL

Antarctica Service Medal

Bronze, Gold, or Silver

Service: All Services
Instituted: 1960
Dates: 1946 to Present
Criteria: 30 calendar days of service on the Antarctic Continent
Devices: Bronze, gold, silver disks (denote bars below)
Bars: "Wintered Over" in bronze, gold, silver

Authorized on July 7, 1960 and awarded to any member of the Armed Forces who, from January 2, 1946, is a member of a direct support or exploratory operation in Antarctica; includes Air Force personnel who participate in flights supporting operations in Antarctica. A "WINTERED OVER" clasp is worn on the medal and a disc with the outline of the continent is worn on the ribbon bar if the individual remains on the continent during the winter months. (First stay — bronze disc; second stay — gold disc; three or more winter tours — silver disc). An appropriately clothed figure is depicted on the front of the medal while the Antarctica continent is depicted on the reverse with the inscription, "COURAGE SACRIFICE DEVOTION."

ARMED FORCES EXPEDITIONARY MEDAL

Armed Forces Expeditionary Medal

Silver

Bronze

Service: All Services
Instituted: 1961
Dates: 1958 to Present
Criteria: Participation in military operations not covered by specific war medal
Devices: All Services: bronze, silver star; Army: bronze arrowhead; Navy: bronze Marine Corps device
Notes: Authorized for service in Vietnam until establishment of Vietnam Service Medal

Authorized on December 4, 1961 to any member of the United States Armed Forces for US military operations, US operations in direct support of the United Nations, and US operations of assistance for friendly foreign nations after July 1, 1958. Operations that qualify for this medal are authorized in specific orders. Participating personnel must have served at least 30 consecutive (60 non-consecutive) days in the qualifying operation or less if the operation was less than 30 days in length. The medal may also be authorized for individuals who do not meet the basic criteria but who do merit special recognition for their service in the designated operation. The first qualifying operation was Operation Blue Bat, a peacekeeping mission in Lebanon from July 1 to November 1, 1958. This medal was initially awarded for Vietnam service between July 1, 1958 and July 3, 1965; an individual awarded this medal for this period of Vietnam service may either keep the award or request the Vietnam Service Medal in lieu of but may not have both awards for Vietnam service. Many personnel received this medal for continuing service in Cambodia after the Vietnam ceasefire. The medal was also authorized for those serving in the Persian Gulf area who previously would have qualified for the Southwest Asia Service Medal and the National Defense Service Medal whose qualification periods for that area terminated on November 30, 1995; individuals who qualify for both the Southwest Asia Service Medal and the Armed Forces Expeditionary Medal must elect to receive the Expeditionary medal. The front of the medal depicts an eagle with wings raised, perched on a sword, in front of a compass rose with eight points; the words "ARMED FORCES EXPEDITIONARY SERVICE" encircle the design. The reverse of the medal shows the presidential shield with branches of laurel below and the inscription, "UNITED STATES OF AMERICA."

VIETNAM SERVICE MEDAL

Silver   Bronze

Service: All Services
Instituted: 1965
Dates: 1965-73
Criteria: Service in Vietnam, Laos, Cambodia or Thailand during the above period
Devices: All Services: bronze, silver star; Army: bronze arrowhead; Navy: bronze Marine Corps device

Authorized by executive order on July 8, 1965 for US military personnel serving in the Vietnam Theater of Operations after July 3, 1965 through March 28, 1973. Personnel must have served in Vietnam on temporary duty for at least 30 consecutive/60 non-consecutive days or have served in combat with a unit directly supporting a military operation in Southeast Asia. Military personnel serving in Laos, Cambodia, or Thailand in direct support of operations in Vietnam are also eligible for this award. Bronze stars are authorized to signify presence during each of the 17 designated campaigns during the inclusive period. (The Armed Forces Expeditionary Medal was awarded for earlier service in Vietnam from July 1, 1958 to July 3, 1965, inclusive; personnel receiving that award may be awarded the Vietnam Service Medal but are not authorized both awards for Vietnam service). Bronze and silver service star attachments are authorized to signify participation in designated campaigns. The front of medal depicts an oriental dragon behind a grove of bamboo trees; below the base of the trees is the inscription "REPUBLIC OF VIETNAM SERVICE." The reverse of the medal depicts a cross bow with a torch through the center and contains the inscription "UNITED STATES OF AMERICA" along the bottom edge. The yellow color of the suspension drape and ribbon represent the color of Vietnam and the Buddhist belief while the three red stripes represent the three ancient Vietnamese empires of Tonkin, Annam, and the Cochin China and the green represents the Vietnam jungle.

The titles of the designated USAF campaigns differ from those of the other services and are listed below. All campaigns except no. 6, the Vietnam Air/Ground Campaign, apply to the entire Theater of Operations which includes Cambodia, Laos, and Vietnam. The overwater battle zone line extends outward to approximately 100 miles from the coast of Vietnam from the northern tip of North Vietnam to the most western tip of South Vietnam (the southwestern portion of South Vietnam).

Designated campaigns for the RVN Campaign Medal are:

1. Vietnam(VN) Advisory - Nov 15, 1961 to Mar 1, 1965
2. VN Defense - Mar 2, 1965 to Jan 30, 1966
3. VN Air Campaign - Jan 31, 1966 to Jun 28, 1966
4. VN Air Offensive Ph I - Jun 29, 1966 to Mar 8, 1967
5. VN Air Offensive Ph II - Mar 9, 1967 to Mar 31, 1968
6. VN Air/Ground Campaign - Jan 22, 1968 to Jun 7, 1968
   (designated campaign area is exclusively Vietnam)
7. VN Air Offensive Ph III - Apr 1, 1968 to Oct 31, 1968
8. VN Air Offensive Ph IV - Nov 1, 1968 to Feb 26, 1969
9. TET 69/Counteroffensive - Feb 23, 1969 to Jun 8, 1969
10. VN Summer-Fall, 69 - Jun 9, 1969 to Oct 31, 1969
11. VN Winter-Spring - Nov 1, 1969 to Apr 30, 1970
12. Sanctuary Counteroffensive - May 1, 1970 to Jun 30, 1970
13. Southwest Monsoon - Jul 1, 1970 to Nov 30, 1970
14. Commando Hunt V - Dec 1, 1970 to May 14, 1971
15. Commando Hunt VI - May 15, 1971 to Oct 31, 1971
16. Commando Hunt VII - Nov 1, 1971 to Mar 29, 1972
17. Vietnam Ceasefire - Mar 30, 1972 to Jan 28, 1973

SOUTHWEST ASIA SERVICE MEDAL

Bronze

Service: All Services
Instituted: 1992
Dates: 1991 to 1995
Criteria: Active participation in, or support of, Operations Desert Shield and/or Desert Storm
Devices: All Services: bronze star; Navy: bronze Marine Corps device

Awarded to members of the United States Armed Forces who participated in or directly supported military operations in Southwest Asia or in surrounding areas between August 2, 1990 and November 30, 1995 (Operations Desert Shield and Desert Storm). The medal was established by and executive order signed by President George Bush on March 15, 1991. There were three campaign periods for the Gulf War; each is represented by a bronze star attachment. The front of the medal contains aircraft, helicopter, tank, armored personnel carrier, tent and troops, battleship in both desert and sea setting along with the inscription "SOUTHWEST ASIA SERVICE." The reverse of the medal contains a sword entwined with a palm leaf and the inscription "UNITED STATES OF AMERICA."

The three designated campaigns for the Southwest Asia Service Medal are:

1. The Defense of Saudia Arabia -- August 2, 1990 - January 16, 1991
2. The Liberation and Defense of Kuwait -- January 17, 1991 - April 11, 1991
3. The Southwest Asia Cease Fire Campaign -- April 12, 1991 - November 30, 1995.

ARMED FORCES SERVICE MEDAL

Armed Forces Service Medal

Silver   Bronze

Service: All Services
Instituted: 1995
Dates: 1995 to Present
Criteria: Participation in military operations not covered by a specific war medal or the Armed Forces Expeditionary Medal
Devices: All Services: bronze, silver star

Authorized on January 11, 1996 for U.S. military personnel who on or after June 1, 1992 participate in a U.S. military operation deemed to be significant activity in which no foreign armed opposition or imminent hostile action is encountered and for which no previous U.S. service medal is authorized. The medal can be awarded to service members in direct support of the United Nations or North Atlantic Treaty Organization, and for assistance operations to friendly nations. The initial awards of this medal were for operations that have occurred in the Balkans since 1992. Qualifications include at least one day of participation in the designated area. Direct support of the operation and aircraft flights within the area also qualify for award of this medal as long as at least one day is served within the designated area. Bronze service stars are worn on the medal and ribbon for each succeeding operation justifying an award of this medal. Recent operations that qualify for the medal are Provide Promise, Joint Endeavor, Able Sentry, Deny Flight, Maritime Monitor, and Sharp Guard. The front of the medal identifies the medal and has the torch of liberty within its center; the reverse of the medal has the American eagle with the U.S. shield in its chest and spread wings clutching three arrows in its talons encircled by a laurel wreath and the inscription, "IN PURSUIT OF DEMOCRACY."

HUMANITARIAN SERVICE MEDAL

Silver   Bronze

Service: All Services
Instituted: 1977
Dates: 1975 to Present
Criteria: Direct participation in specific operations of a humanitarian nature
Devices: All Services: bronze, silver star; Army/Air Force/Navy Marine Corps: bronze numeral (obsolete)

Authorized on January 19, 1977 and awarded to Air Force personnel (including Reserve components), who subsequent to April 1, 1975, distinguished themselves by meritorious direct participation in a DOD approved significant military act or operation of a humanitarian nature. According to Air Force regulations, the participation must be "hands-on" at the site of the operation; personnel assigned to staff functions geographically separated from the operation are not eligible for this medal. Service members must be assigned and/or attached to participating units for specific operations by official orders. Members who were present for duty at specific qualifying locations for the medal but who did not make a direct contribution to the action or operation are specifically excluded from eligibility. Recent qualifying events for this medal include the Hurricane Fran Disaster Relief Operation (September 5 - 13, 1996), the Oklahoma City Bombing Disaster Relief Operation (April 19 - May 3, 1995) and the Southeast Flood Disaster Relief Operation (July - Aug, 1994). A recent example of a unit being awarded this medal was the 9th Reconnaissance Wing at Beale AFB, California who provided shelter, food, security, and medical assistance to over 8,000 people during the flooding around the Yuba and Feather Rivers during the period January 1-6, 1997. The front of the medal depicts a right hand with open palm within a circle; the reverse contains an oak sprig and the inscriptions "FOR HUMANITARIAN SERVICE" and "UNITED STATES ARMED FORCES." Bronze numeral attachments are authorized for additional awards.

OUTSTANDING VOLUNTEER SERVICE MEDAL

Silver   Bronze

Service: All Services
Instituted: 1993
Dates: 1993 to Present
Criteria: Awarded for outstanding and sustained voluntary service to the civilian community
Devices: bronze, silver star

Authorized in 1993 to members of the U.S. Armed Forces and reserve components. Awarded for outstanding and sustained voluntary service to the civilian community after December 31, 1992. It may be awarded to active duty and reserve members who perform outstanding volunteer service over time as opposed to a single event. The service performed must have been to the civilian community and must be strictly voluntary and not duty-related. The volunteerism must be of a sustained and direct nature and must be significant and produce tangible results while reflecting favorably on the Air Force and the Department of Defense. There are no specific time requirements as to how many hours must be spent on the volunteer activity, but the activity should consist of significant action and involvement rather than, for example, simply attending meetings as a member of a community service group. An individual would normally be considered for only one award during an assignment. Group-level commanders, including commanders of provisional and composite groups, have approval authority for the medal. Bronze and silver stars are authorized attachments to denote additional awards. The front of the bronze medal has a five-pointed star with a circular ring over each point; the star, a symbol of the military and representing outstanding service, is encircled by a laurel wreath which represents honor and achievement. The reverse has an oak leaf branch, symbolic of strength and potential, with three oak leaves and two acorns along with the inscriptions, "OUTSTANDING VOLUNTEER SERVICE," and "UNITED   STATES ARMED FORCES."

ARMED FORCES RESERVE MEDAL

2
Numeral

Bronze, Silver and Gold Hourglass

Bronze

Service: All Services
Instituted: 1950
Dates: 1949 to Present
Criteria: 10 years of honorable service in any reserve component of the United States Armed Forces Reserve or award of "M" device
Devices: Bronze, silver and gold hourglass, bronze letter "M"

Authorized in 1950 for 10 years of honorable and satisfactory service within a 12 year period as a member of one or more of the Reserve Components of the Armed Forces of the United States. Creditable service prior to July 1, 1949 must be with Reserve components listed in appropriate Air Force regulations; creditable service after that date involves specified accumulation of retirement points.

An Executive Order on Aug 8, 1996 authorized the award of the bronze "M" mobilization device to U.S. reserve component members who have performed qualifying active-duty service in support of a designated contingency operation on or after August 1, 1990 (the M device was not authorized for any operations previous to August 1, 1990 although initial proposals had mentioned that it might be). Units called up in support of Operations Desert Storm/Desert Shield are the first units to be authorized the "M" device; the first two "M" devices were awarded by Defense Secretary Wiliam Perry on August 29, 1996 to two Air Force Reservists from the 459th Airlift Wing at Andrews AFB, Maryland. Almost 3,000 National Guard and Reserve (including Air Force) personnel, who were mobilized for the Persian Gulf war, Operation Restore Hope (Somalia), Operation Uphold Democracy (Haiti), and Operation Joint Endeavor (Bosnia) were eligible for the "M." The device is worn on the medal and ribbon.

If an "M" is awarded, it is awarded with the medal even though service might be less than 10 years. Numerals beginning with "2" are authorized to be worn to the right of the bronze "M"on the ribbon bar or below the "M" on the medal, indicating the total number of times the individual was mobilized.

Bronze, silver, gold hourglasses are awarded for 10, 20, 30 years service, respectively. Previous to this change, only bronze hourglasses were awarded at each successive 10 year point (first hourglass at 20 year point).

The front of the medal depicts a flaming torch placed vertically between a crossed bugle and powder horn; thirteen stars and thirteen rays surround the design. The front of the medal is the same for all services; only the back design is different. The Air Force design on the reverse is an eagle with wings spread in front of a circle with clouds and includes the inscription "ARMED FORCES RESERVE." Air Force National Guard members who qualify for this medal are authorized the medal with the National Guard insignia on the reverse —eagle with crossed cannons in its center.

The reverse of the medal for other services is as follows:
Army -- has a Minuteman in front of a circle with 13 stars representing the original colonies
Navy -- has a sailing ship with an anchor on its front with an eagle with wings spread superimposed upon it
Marine Corps -- has the USMC emblem, eagle, globe, and anchor
Coast Guard -- has the Coast Guard emblem, crossed anchor with the Coast Guard shield in the center

AIR FORCE OVERSEAS (SHORT TOUR) RIBBON

Overseas Service Ribbon - Short Tour

Silver   Bronze

Service: Air Force
Instituted: 1980
Criteria: Successful completion of an overseas tour designated
as "short term" by appropriate authority
Devices: Bronze, silver oak leaf cluster

Authorized on October 12, 1980. Awarded to Air Force active duty, Reserve, and National Guard personnel who have been awarded credit for a short overseas tour after September 1, 1980. Individual must have been on active status as of the institution date to qualify for this ribbon; an individual who may have earned short tour credit in 1970, for example, would be eligible for this ribbon if he/she were still on active duty in 1980. To receive short tour credit, an individual must spend at least 15 months overseas; short tour credit can also be awarded if the individual accumulates 300 days of temporary duty overseas in an 18 month period. Additional short tour credits are represented by oak leaf clusters.

AIR FORCE OVERSEAS (LONG TOUR) RIBBON

Overseas Service Ribbon - Long Tour

Silver   Bronze

Service: Air Force
Instituted: 1980
Criteria: Successful completion of an overseas tour designated
as "long term" by appropriate authority
Devices: Bronze, silver oak leaf cluster

Authorized on October 12, 1980. Awarded to Air Force active duty, Reserve and National Guard personnel who have been awarded credit for a long overseas tour after September 1, 1980. Individual must have been on active status as of the institution date to qualify for this ribbon. Long tour credit is awarded for an assignment of at least 24 months overseas; credit for a long tour may be also be awarded for accumulating 365 days of temporary duty overseas in a three year period. A consecutive tour overseas would entitle an individual to an oak leaf cluster for an additional award of this ribbon. Additional nonconsecutive tours are also represented by oak leaf clusters. The ribbon may be awarded retroactively to those personnel who were on active duty as of the institution date.

AIR FORCE LONGEVITY SERVICE AWARD RIBBON

Longevity Service Award Ribbon

Silver   Bronze

Service: Air Force
Instituted: 1957
Criteria: Successful completion of an aggregate total of four
years of honorable active service
Devices: Bronze, silver oak leaf cluster

Awarded to U.S. Air Force personnel for 4 years honorable active federal military service with any branch of the U.S. Armed Forces or reserve components. Reserve and Guard require 4 years creditable service for retirement. Additional 4 years' creditable service is denoted by an oak leaf cluster attachment. As an example, an individual who retires at 20 years service would have 4 bronze oak leaf clusters on the ribbon. Individuals on active duty as of the institution date are authorized to wear the appropriate attachments to properly reflect their service both prior to and after that date. Individuals who served both in the Army Air Force and continued their service into the U.S. Air Force until 1957 or later would be authorized to wear the Longevity Service Award with appropriate oak leaf clusters to properly represent their total service during both periods.

NCO PROFESSIONAL MILITARY EDUCATION GRADUATE RIBBON

NCO Professional Mil. Education Grad. Ribbon

Silver   Bronze

Service: Air Force
Instituted: 1962
Criteria: Successful completion of a certified NCO professional military education school
Devices: Bronze, silver oak leaf cluster

Authorized on August 28, 1962. Awarded to graduates of Non-commissioned Officer Professional Military Education (PME) courses to include the NCO Preparatory Course, Airman Leadership School, NCO Leadership School, NCO Academy, and Sr. NCO Academy. Successive levels of PME are denoted by the addition of an oak leaf cluster attachment.

USAF BASIC MILITARY TRAINING (BMT) HONOR GRADUATE RIBBON

Basic Military Training Honor Graduate Ribbon

None

Service: Air Force
Instituted: 1976
Criteria: Demonstration of excellence in all academic and military training phases of basic Air Force entry training
Devices: None

Authorized on April 3, 1976. Awarded to USAF Basic Military Training (BMT) honor graduates after July 29, 1976, according to criteria established by Air Education and Training Command (previously, Air Training Command).

SMALL ARMS EXPERT MARKSMANSHIP RIBBON

Small Arms Expert Marksmanship Ribbon

Bronze

Service: Air Force
Instituted: 1962
Criteria: Qualification as expert with either the M-16 rifle or standard Air Force issue handgun
Devices: Bronze star

Authorized on August 28, 1962. Awarded to Air Force personnel who, after 1 Jan 1963, qualify as expert with either the M16 rifle or issue handgun on the Air Force qualification course or on a prescribed course or who completes the Combat Rifle Program. The ribbon is only awarded once regardless of how many times an individual qualifies as "expert." A bronze star device is added (only once) if the award criteria is met with both the rifle and handgun.

AIR FORCE TRAINING RIBBON

Air Force Training Ribbon

Silver   Bronze

Service: Air Force
Instituted: 1980
Criteria: Successful completion of an Air Force accession training program
Devices: Bronze, silver oak leaf cluster

Authorized on October 12, 1980. Awarded to Air Force members who complete an Air Force accession training program after August 14, 1974 such as Basic Military Training(BMT), Officer Training School (OTS), Reserve Officer Training Corps (ROTC), USAF Academy, Medical Services, Judge Advocate, Chaplain orientation and so forth. Also authorized for Guard and Reserve members who complete the appropriate training program. If a member completes two accession training programs, such as BMT and OTS, a bronze oak leaf cluster is worn on the ribbon. Award is retroactive for those personnel on active duty as of the authorization date.

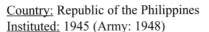

PHILIPPINE DEFENSE MEDAL

Country: Republic of the Philippines
Instituted: 1945 (Army: 1948)
Criteria: Service in defense of the Philippines between 8 December 1941
and 15 June 1942
Devices: Bronze star

Authorized in 1944 and awarded to members of the US Armed Forces for service in the defense of the Philippines from December 8, 1941 to June 15, 1942. Established by the Philippine army, this was originally a ribbon only award. To qualify for the medal, personnel must have participated in any engagement against the enemy in Philippine territory, in Philippine waters, or in the air over the Philippines or Philippine waters. The medal was designed in 1948. A bronze service star is authorized for members of the Bataan or Manila Bay forces and for participation in an engagement or for assignment in Philippine territory or waters for not less than 30 days. The front of the bronze medallion depicts a Philippine female warrior with sword and shield; three stars representing Luzon, Visayan, and Mindanao are centered above her head along with a floral design on the left and a map of Corregidor and Bataan on the bottom right. The green wreath represents the lesser islands. The reverse of the medal contains the inscription, "FOR THE DEFENSE OF THE PHILIPPINES." The red of the ribbon represents courage and the white represents liberty.

PHILIPPINE LIBERATION MEDAL

Country: Republic of the Philippines
Instituted: 1945 (Army: 1948)
Criteria: Service in the liberation of the Philippines between 17 October
1944 and 3 September 1945
Devices: Bronze star

Authorized in 1945 and awarded to members of the US Armed Forces for service in the liberation of the Philippines from October 17, 1944 to September 3, 1945. Personnel must have participated in the initial landing operations on Leyte or adjoining islands from October 17, 1944 to October 20, 1944, participated in any engagement against the enemy during the campaign on Leyte and adjoining islands, participated in any engagement on any other Philippine island, or served in the Philippine Islands or in ships in Philippine waters for not less than 30 days during the period. A maximum of 3 bronze service stars, each representing one of the qualifying conditions for the medal, were authorized for this medal. The front of the gold-colored medal is in the shape of arched wings which contain a sword superimposed on a white shield that has three gold stars at its top and a gold band with the word "LIBERTY" going through it. The blue, white, and red enamel on the shield as well as the colors of the ribbon symbolizes courage, liberty, and perseverence. The three stars on the top of the shield represent Luzon, Visayan, and the Mindanao Islands. The reverse of the medal contains the inscription, "FOR THE LIBERATION OF THE PHILIPPINES."

PHILIPPINE INDEPENDENCE MEDAL

Country: Republic of the Philippines
Instituted: 1946 (Army: 1948)
Criteria: Receipt of both the Philippine Defense and Liberation Medals/Ribbons. Originally presented to those present for duty in the Philippines on 4 July 1946
Devices: None

Authorized in 1946. Current regulations state that an individual must be awarded the Philippine Defense Medal and the Philippine Liberation Medal to be authorized this medal. AAF regulations of the period indicate that an individual must have been serving in the Philippines on 4 July 1946 to qualify for this medal. It appears that the original intent of the medal was to recognize those who served in either the Defense period (Dec 8, 1941 - Jun 15, 1942) or the Liberation period (Oct 17, 1944 - Sep 3, 1945) which both obviously contributed to the eventual liberation and independence of the Philippines. There would not have been many personnel who would have served in the Philippines during both periods, which were 2-3 years apart. No attachments are authorized for this medal. Separation papers from World War II that can be found indicate award of the Liberation medal only and some indicate award of the Liberation and Independence medals without mention of the Philippine Defense Medal. The front of the medal contains a native female figure holding the staff of the Philippine flag while flanked by two rows of other flags representing the nations of the world. The inscriptions, "PHILIPPINE INDEPENDENCE" and "JULY 4, 1946" are separated by two five-pointed stars. The back reads "Granted Philippine Independence by the United States of America." The ribbon colors are white, red, blue, and yellow, representing liberty, courage, and perseverance with independence.

FOREIGN DECORATIONS

(Republic of Vietnam Gallantry Cross Medal with Palm is shown as an example. The ribbon chest on page 80 shows the Republic of Vietnam Armed Forces Honor Medal as the example.)

Decorations from a foreign country are not worn unless you wear other US military decorations and service medals. If an individual is authorized decorations from more than one country, he/she should wear them in the order earned; for more than one decoration from the same country, wear them in the order of precedence established by that country. The Republic of Vietnam Gallantry Cross with palm is shown as an example; the palm attachment signifies that it was awarded at the Armed Forces level. This medal was often awarded by the Republic of Vietnam for valorous service in combat during the Vietnam war. Other authorized attachments are bronze star for award at Brigade and Regiment level, silver star for award at Division level and a gold star for award at Corps level. Many veterans of the Vietnam War often confuse this medal with the RVN Gallantry Cross Unit Citation which has the identical ribbon except it is enclosed in a gold frame. This unit citation is often listed on the DD214 as RVN Gallantry Cross Unit Citation. To properly denote award of the medal, the ribbon bar should be worn without the gold frame since that indicates award of a unit citation. For more detailed information on Repubic of Vietnam awards see _The Decorations and Medals of the Republic of Vietnam and Her Allies, 1950 - 1975._

REPUBLIC OF THE PHILIPPINES PRESIDENTIAL UNIT CITATION

Service: All Services
Instituted: 1948
Criteria: Awarded to units of the U.S. Armed Forces for service in
the war against Japan and/or for 1970 and 1972 disaster relief
Devices: All Services (except Army) Bronze star

Awarded to units serving in the Philippines from December 7, 1941 to May 10, 1942 and from October 17, 1944 to July 4, 1945. In most cases, individuals who received the Philippine Liberation Medal were also awarded this presidential unit citation. Individuals should check appropriate service unit records to verify entitlement if not so indicated on individual separation documents. The ribbon was also awarded for disaster relief operations in the Philippines during July and August 1972. A gold-colored frame encloses the ribbon.

REPUBLIC OF KOREA PRESIDENTIAL UNIT CITATION

Service: All Services
Instituted: 1951
Criteria: Awarded to certain units of the U.S. Armed Forces for
services rendered during the Korean War
Devices: None

Awarded by the President of the Republic of Korea to units serving in Korean military operations during the Korean Conflict from 1950 to 1954. While most units involved in the Korean War received this recognition, individuals should check official unit records to verify qualification for the award. Also awarded for disaster relief operations during August 19-20, 1972. No attachments authorized. A gold-colored frame encloses the ribbon.

FOREIGN UNIT CITATIONS

The Republic of Vietnam Gallantry Cross Unit Citation with Palm

The Republic of Vietnam Civil Action Unit Citation with Palm

Unit citations from a foreign country should not be worn unless other US military decorations and service medals are worn. They should be worn in the correct precedence established by the awarding country and if from more than one country they should be worn in the order earned. A gold-colored frame is usually worn on the unit citation.

The Republic of Vietnam Gallantry Cross Citation with Palm and the Republic of Vietnam Civil Action Unit Citation with Palm are shown as examples. The Gallantry Cross Citation was awarded by the Republic of Vietnam to recognize the achievements or service of units serving in the Vietnam Military Operation in recognition of valorous achievement in combat from March 1, 1961- 1973. Cited units are noted in Air Force regulations. The Republic of Vietnam Civil Action Citation with Palm was awarded in recognition of meritorious civil action service.

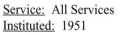

UNITED NATIONS (KOREAN) SERVICE MEDAL

Service: All Services

Instituted: 1951

Criteria: Service on behalf of the United Nations in Korea between 27 June 1950 and 27 July 1954

Devices: None

Notes: Above date denotes when award was authorized for wear by U.S. military personnel

Established by the UN General Assembly on December 12, 1950. Presidential acceptance was announced on November 27, 1951. Awarded to U.S. military personnel for service in the Korean Theater in support of the United Nations Command between 27 June 1950 and 27 July 1954. Personnel awarded the Korean Service Medal automatically establish eligibility for this medal. The front of the medal shows a polar projection map of the world encircled by olive branches; a permanent bar with the word "KOREA" is centered across the lower portion of the medal drape. The reverse of the medal bears the inscription "FOR SERVICE IN DEFENSE OF THE PRINCIPLES OF THE CHARTER OF THE UNITED NATIONS." There are no attachments authorized for the medal and ribbon bar.

UNITED NATIONS MEDAL

Service: All Services

Instituted: 1964

Criteria: 6 months' service with any of the following UN operations: UNTSO, UNOGIL, UNMOGIP or UNSFH

Devices: Bronze star

Notes: Above date denotes when award was authorized for wear by U.S. military personnel

Established by the Secretary General of the UN on July 30, 1959 and accepted by the President for US Armed Forces on March 11, 1964. Awarded for six months' service in a UN operation. Individuals should wear the first UN medal with unique suspension and the service ribbon for which they qualify; for involvement in subsequent operations, a bronze service star is affixed to the medal drape and the service ribbon. One of the most recent UN medals authorized for Air Force personnel is the United Nations Mission in Haiti Medal which was authorized for Air Force members who served under the operational or tactical control of the United Nations in Haiti for at least 90 consecutive days. The UN medal is the same design for all authorized operations; however, the ribbon color will be different for each UN operation. The front of the medal depicts the United Nations emblem, a polar projection of the world with the North Pole at its center and a wreath of olive leaves encircling the emblem with the letters "UN" at the top. The reverse of the medal has the inscription, "IN THE SERVICE OF PEACE."

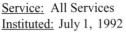

NATO MEDAL

Service: All Services

Instituted: July 1, 1992

Criteria: 30 days service in or 90 days outside the former Republic of Yugoslavia and the Adriatic Sea under NATO command and in direct support of NATO operations.

Devices: None

Notes: Above date denotes when award was authorized for wear by U.S. military personnel

Awarded to U.S. military personnel who served 30 days or 90 days outside of the former Republic of Yugoslavia and the Adriatic Sea. Must have served between July 1, 1992 to a date currently undetermined under NATO command and in direct support of NATO operations. The medal may be presented with a service clasp indicating the theater of operations, i.e. Yugoslavia bar that is attached to the drape of the medal. U.S. military personnel may accept the medal this way but may only wear the basic medal and service ribbon without the clasp. The first Air Force personnel to be presented with the award was Master Sergeant Barbara Wright while assigned to Ramstein Air Base and deployed to Zagreb, Croatia, as part of Operation Provide Promise, for establishing mail-support operations for forces assigned to Bosnia and the Republic of Yugoslavia. The front of the bronze medal bears the NATO star set in a wreath of olive leaves. The reverse of the medal contains the inscription "NORTH ATLANTIC TREATY ORGANIZATION" in both English and French along the outer rim of the medal. In the center area of the medal is the inscription "IN SERVICE OF PEACE AND FREEDOM" also in both English and French. Subsequent awards are denoted by a bronze service star.

MULTINATIONAL FORCE & OBSERVERS MEDAL

Service: All Services

Instituted: 1982

Criteria: 6 months service with the Multinational Force & Observers peacekeeping force in the Sinai Desert

Devices: Bronze numeral

Notes: Above date denotes when award was authorized for wear by U.S. military personnel

Established on 24 March 1982 for personnel who have served at least 90 days with the Multinational Force and Observers after 3 August 1981. As of 15 March 1985, 170 days minimum service is required for the award. The medal was designed to recognize those who participated in the Mideast peacekeeping force. The front of the medal depicts a dove and olive branch while the reverse has the inscription "UNITED IN SERVICE FOR PEACE." Bronze numerals are authorized for the medal and ribbon for subsequent awards.

Inter-American Defense Board Medal

Service: All Services
Instituted: 1982
Criteria: Service with the Inter-American Defense Board for at least one year
Devices: Gold star
Notes: Above date denotes when award was authorized for wear by U.S. military personnel

The medal and ribbon were established by the Inter-American Defense Board on December 11, 1945 and authorized by Executive Order on January 18, 1969. DOD authorized the acceptance and wearing of the medal and ribbon by members of the U.S. Armed Forces on May 12, 1981. Awarded for permanent wear to military personnel who have served on the Inter-American Defense Board for at least one year as either chairman of the board, delegates, advisers, officers of the staff, officers of the secretariat, or officers of the Inter-American Defense College. U.S. military personnel who have been awarded the medal and ribbon may wear them when attending meetings, ceremonies, or other functions where Latin American members of the Board are present. The front of the medal has the flags of the nations of the western hemisphere surrounding a projection of that area.

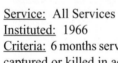

Republic of Vietnam Campaign Medal with Date Bar

Service: All Services
Instituted: 1966
Criteria: 6 months service in the Republic of Vietnam between 1961 and 1973 or if wounded, captured or killed in action during the above period
Devices: Silver date bar
Notes: Bar inscribed "1960" is the only authorized version

Authorized on 20 June 1966, as amended on 31 January 1974. Awarded by the Republic of Vietnam to US military personnel who have served at least 6 months in the Republic of Vietnam between 1 March 1961 and 28 March 1973 or who have provided direct combat support to the Republic of Vietnam Armed Forces during the period of award while stationed in areas outside of Vietnam, such as Laos, Thailand, and Guam. In most cases, an individual who qualified for the Vietnam Service Medal would also qualify for this medal since most personnel spent at least six months in the theater or in direct support of the operation. Medal and ribbon should come with a silver attachment with the inscription, "1960- "; other devices that include an ending date for the award are unofficial. The ending date is blank since the government of Vietnam no longer exists as a republic. Many examples of date bars with an ending date are seen on Vietnam Campaign medals awarded in the mid to late 1960's. The front of the medal is a six-pointed white star superimposed against a sunburst design; the center of the star has a design in the shape of Vietnam in the center of a green enameled circle.

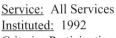

SAUDI ARABIA LIBERATION OF KUWAIT MEDAL

Service: All Services
Instituted: 1992
Criteria: Participation in, or support of, Operation Desert Storm (1991)
Devices: Gold palm tree device
Notes: Support must have been performed in theater (e.g.: Persian Gulf, Red Sea, Iraq, Kuwait, Saudi Arabia, Gulf of Oman, etc.)

Instituted in 1992 and authorized to U.S. military personnel who participated in Desert Storm or who, while in the theater of operations, provided support of Desert Storm operations during the period January 17, 1991-February 28, 1991. The medal has an elaborate and complex design; it depicts the country of Kuwait in the center of a bronze disk that has a crown at its top with the ends of two encircling palm branches meeting on each of its sides. At the bottom of this disk are the words "LIBERATION OF KUWAIT" in both Arabic and English; the top of the disk has two crossed swords with a palm tree in their center. This entire bronze area is centered on a star of 15 large and 15 smaller silver rays, all with rounded edges. The ribbon bar has a palm tree with crossed swords as the only authorized attachment. Individuals who qualify for this medal also are eligible for the Kuwait Liberation of Kuwait Medal as well as the National Defense Service Medal and the Southwest Asia Service Medal.

KUWAIT LIBERATION OF KUWAIT MEDAL

Service: All Services
Instituted: 1995
Criteria: Participation in, or support of, Operations Desert Shield and/or Desert Storm (1990-93)
Devices: None
Notes: Above date denotes when award was authorized for wear by U.S. military personnel

Offered by the Kuwait government to members of the Armed Forces of the United States in July 1994 and accepted by the Secretary of Defense in March 1995. Awarded for service in Desert Shield/ Desert Storm during the period August 2,1990 to Aug 31, 1993. Personnel must have served for one day or more in a ground and/or shore operation, one day or more with a naval vessel, in one or more aerial flights, or on temporary duty for 30 consecutive/60 non-consecutive days during the designated period in support of military operations in the area (The time requirement can be waived if individual participated in combat operations). The time period for this medal is less restrictive than the Saudi Arabia Liberation of Kuwait Medal. The front of the medal bears the Coat of Arms of the State of Kuwait. Individuals who qualify for the Southwest Asia Service Medal and the Saudia Arabia Liberation of Kuwait Medal are also eligible for the Kuwait Liberation of Kuwait Medal. The Coat of Arms consists of the shield of the flag design superimposed on a falcon with wings spread. The falcon supports a disk which contains a sailing ship with the full name of the state written above it. At the top of the medal written in Arabic is the inscription "1991 Liberation Medal." On the reverse of the medal is a map of Kuwait on a rayed background. No attachments are authorized for the medal or ribbon.

United Nations Medals Authorized for Award to United States Air Force Personnel

Until recently Air Force personnel serving on or with a United Nations mission were permitted to wear only two UN medals. The two medals were the UN medal for Korea or the UNTSO (UN Truce Supervision Organization) medal.

A change to Department of Defense regulations now authorizes military personnel to wear the ribbon of the mission in which they served. Only one UN ribbon may be worn. Additional missions or awards of UN medals are indicated by a bronze star.

The 15 UN missions the United States has participated in are listed below :

1. UNTSO United Nations Truce Supervision Organization June 1948 to present.
2. UNMOGIP United Nations Military Observer Group in India and Pakistan, Jan. 1949 to present.
3.KOREA United Nations Korean Service, June 1950 to July 1953.
4. UNSF, United Nations Security Force in West New Guinea (West Irian).Also: United Nations Temporary Executive Authority, Oct 1962 to April 1963.
5. UNIKOM United Nations Iraq-Kuwait Observation Mission June 1991 to Feb 1995.
6. MINURSO United Nations Mission for the Referendum in Western Sahara (acronym derives from the French: **MI**ssion des **N**ations **U**nies pour le **R**eferendum dans le **Sa**hara **O**ccidental) Sept 1991 to present.
7. UNAMIC United Nations Advance Mission in Cambodia, OCt 1991 to Mar 1992.
8. UNPROFOR United Nations Protection Force (in the Former Yugoslavia) March 1992 to Dec. 1995.
9. UNTAC United Nations Transitional Authority in Cambodia March 1992 to Sept 1993.
10. UNOSOM II United Nations Operation in Somalia II, May 1993 to Mar 1993.
11. UNOMIG United Nations Observer Mission in Georgia Aug. 1993 to present.
12. UNMIH United Nations Mission in Haiti, Sept 1993 to June 1996.
13. UNCRO United Nations Confidence Restoration Operation in Croatia, March 1995 to Jan 1996.
14. UNPREDEP United Nations Preventive Deployment Force (Former Yugoslavia), Mar 1995 to present.
15. UNMIBH United Nations Mission in Bosnia and Herzegovina, Dec. 1995 to present.

UNTSO - United Nations Truce Supervision Organization

COUNTRY/LOCATION: Palestine/Israel

DATES: June 1948 to present

COUNTRIES PARTICIPATING: (20) Argentina, Australia, Austria, Belgium, Canada, Chile, China, Denmark, Finland, France, Ireland, Italy, Myanmar, Netherlands, New Zealand, Norway, Sweden, Switzerland, United States, USSR

MAXIMUM STRENGTH: 572 military observers (1948)

CURRENT STRENGTH: 178 (1996)

FATALITIES: 38 (1996)   CLASP(S): **CONGO, UNGOMAP, OSGAP**

This was the first observer mission of the United Nations and, chronologically speaking, is the longest-running. It was formed in 1948 as a step towards the establishment and maintenance of a cease-fire during the first Arab-Israeli conflict.

UNMOGIP - United Nations Military Observer Group in India and Pakistan

COUNTRY/LOCATION: India, Pakistan (Jammu & Kashmir)

DATES: January 1949 to present

COUNTRIES PARTICIPATING: (15) Australia, Belgium, Canada, Chile, Denmark, Ecuador, Finland, Italy, Korean Republic, Mexico, New Zealand, Norway, Sweden, United States, Uruguay

MAXIMUM STRENGTH: 102 military observers (1965)

CURRENT STRENGTH: 44 (1996)

FATALITIES: 9 (1996)

CLASP(S): None

KOREA - United Nations Korean Service

COUNTRY/LOCATION: Korea   DATES: June 1950 to July 1953

COUNTRIES PARTICIPATING: (19) Australia, Belgium, Canada, Colombia, Ethiopia, France, Greece, Luxembourg, Netherlands, New Zealand, Philippines, South Korea, Thailand, Turkey, Union of South Africa, United Kingdom, United States (plus Denmark and Italy which provided medical support)

MAXIMUM STRENGTH (approx): 1,000,000 (UN & South Korea combined)

CURRENT STRENGTH: --------

FATALITIES (approx): Korea: 415,000, U.S.: 55,000, Other UN: 3,100   CLASP(S): None

UNSF - United Nations Security Force in West New Guinea (West Irian)
UNTEA - United Nations Temporary Executive Authority

COUNTRY/LOCATION: West Irian (West New Guinea)

DATES: October 1962 to April 1963

COUNTRIES PARTICIPATING: (9) Brazil, Canada, Ceylon, India, Ireland, Nigeria, Pakistan, Sweden, United States

MAXIMUM STRENGTH: 1,576 military observers (1963)

STRENGTH AT WITHDRAWAL: 1,576

FATALITIES: None   CLASP(S): None

UNIKOM - United Nations Iraq-Kuwait Observation Mission

COUNTRY/LOCATION: Iraq, Kuwait

DATES: April 1991 to present

COUNTRIES PARTICIPATING: (36) Argentina, Austria, Bangladesh, Canada, Chile, China, Denmark, Fiji, Finland, France, Germany, Ghana, Greece, Hungary, India, Indonesia, Ireland, Italy, Kenya, Malaysia, Nigeria, Norway, Pakistan, Poland, Romania, Russian Federation, Senegal, Singapore, Sweden, Switzerland, Thailand, Turkey, United Kingdom, United States, Uruguay, Venezuela

MAXIMUM STRENGTH: 1,187 military observers

CURRENT STRENGTH: 1,179 (1996)

FATALITIES: 6 (1996)   CLASP(S): None

MINURSO - United Nations Mission for the Referendum in Western Sahara

COUNTRY/LOCATION: Western Sahara (Morocco)

DATES: September 1991 to present

COUNTRIES PARTICIPATING: (36) Argentina, Australia, Austria, Bangladesh, Belgium, Canada, China, Egypt, El Salvador, Finland, France, Germany, Ghana, Greece, Guinea-Bissau, Honduras, Hungary, Ireland, Italy, Kenya, Korean Republic, Malaysia, Nigeria, Norway, Pakistan, Peru, Poland, Portugal, Russian Federation, Switzerland, Togo, Tunisia, United Kingdom, United States, Uruguay, Venezuela

MAXIMUM STRENGTH: 3,000 authorized (1,700 military observers and troops, 300 police officers, approx. 1,000 civilian personnel)

CURRENT STRENGTH: 352 (1996)

FATALITIES: 7 (1996)   CLASP(S): None

UNAMIC - United Nations Advance Mission in Cambodia

COUNTRY/LOCATION: Cambodia

DATES: November 1991 to March 1992

COUNTRIES PARTICIPATING: (24) Algeria, Argentina, Australia, Austria, Belgium, Canada, China, France, Germany, Ghana, India, Indonesia, Ireland, Malaysia, New Zealand, Pakistan, Poland, Russian Federation, Senegal, Thailand, Tunisia, United Kingdom, United States, Uruguay

MAXIMUM STRENGTH: 1,090 military and civilian personnel (1992)

STRENGTH AT TRANSITION TO UNTAC: 1,090

FATALITIES: None

UNPROFOR - United Nations Protection Force

COUNTRY/LOCATION: Former Yugoslavia (Bosnia, Herzegovina, Croatia, Serbia, Montenegro, Macedonia)

DATES: March 1992 to December 1995

COUNTRIES PARTICIPATING: (43) Argentina, Australia, Bangladesh, Belgium, Brazil, Canada, Colombia, Czech Republic, Denmark, Egypt, Finland, France, Germany, Ghana, India, Indonesia, Ireland, Jordan, Kenya, Lithuania, Luxembourg, Malaysia, Nepal, Netherlands, New Zealand, Nigeria, Norway, Pakistan, Poland, Portugal, Russian Federation, Senegal, Slovakia, Spain, Sweden, Switzerland, Thailand, Tunisia, Turkey, Ukraine, United Kingdom, United States, Venezuela

MAXIMUM STRENGTH: 39,922 (38,614 troops and support personnel, 637 military observers, 671 civilian police and 4,058 staff (1994)

STRENGTH AT WITHDRAWAL: 2,675

FATALITIES: 207   CLASP(S): None

UNTAC - United Nations Transitional Authority in Cambodia

LOCATION: Cambodia

DATES: Mar. 1992 to Sept. 1993

COUNTRIES PARTICIPATING: (46) Algeria, Argentina, Australia, Austria, Bangladesh, Belgium, Brunei, Bulgaria, Cameroon, Canada, Chile, China, Colombia, Egypt, Fiji, France, Germany, Ghana, Hungary, India, Indonesia, Ireland, Italy, Japan, Jordan, Kenya, Malaysia, Morocco, Namibia, Nepal, Netherlands, New Zealand, Nigeria, Norway, Pakistan, Philippines, Poland, Russian Federation, Senegal, Singapore, Sweden, Thailand, Tunisia, United Kingdom, United States, Uruguay

MAXIMUM STRENGTH: 19,350 military and civilian personnel (1993)

STRENGTH AT WITHDRAWAL: 2,500 (approx.)

FATALITIES: 78

CLASP(S): **UNAMIC** (later withdrawn)

UNOSOM II - United Nations Operation in Somalia II

COUNTRY/LOCATION: Somalia

DATES: May 1993 to March 1995

COUNTRIES PARTICIPATING: (34) Australia, Bangladesh, Belgium, Botswana, Canada, Egypt, France, Germany, Ghana, Greece, India, Indonesia, Ireland, Italy, Korean Republic, Kuwait, Malaysia, Morocco, Nepal, Netherlands, New Zealand, Nigeria, Norway, Pakistan, Philippines, Romania, Saudi Arabia, Sweden, Tunisia, Turkey, United Arab Emirates, United States, Zambia, Zimbabwe

MAXIMUM STRENGTH: 30,800 authorized (28,000 military personnel and approximately 2,800 civilian staff)

STRENGTH AT WITHDRAWAL: 14,968

FATALITIES: 147   CLASP(S): None

UNOMIG - United Nations Observer Mission in Georgia

COUNTRY/LOCATION: Republic of Georgia

DATES: August 1993 to present

COUNTRIES PARTICIPATING: (23) Albania, Austria, Bangladesh, Cuba, Czech Republic, Denmark, Egypt, France, Germany, Greece, Hungary, Indonesia, Jordan, Korean Republic, Pakistan, Poland, Russian Federation, Sweden, Switzerland, Turkey, United Kingdom, United States, Uruguay

MAXIMUM STRENGTH: 136 military observers (1994)

CURRENT STRENGTH: 128 (1996)

FATALITIES: 2 (1996)   CLASP(S): None

UNMIH - United Nations Mission in Haiti

COUNTRY/LOCATION: Haiti

DATES: Sept 1993 to June 1996

COUNTRIES PARTICIPATING: (34) Algeria, Antigua and Barbuda, Argentina, Austria, Bahamas, Bangladesh, Barbados, Belize, Benin, Canada, Djibouti, France, Guatemala, Guinea-Bissau, Guyana, Honduras, India, Ireland, Jamaica, Jordan, Mali. Nepal, Netherlands, New Zealand, Pakistan, Philippines, Russian Federation, St.Kitts & Nevis, St.Lucia, Suriname, Togo, Trinidad and Tobago, Tunisia, United States

MAXIMUM STRENGTH: 6,065 military personnel and 847 civilian police (1995)

STRENGTH AT TRANSITION TO UNSMIH: 1,200 troops and 300 civilian police

FATALITIES: 6   CLASP(S): None

UNCRO - United Nations Confidence Restoration Operation in Croatia

COUNTRY/LOCATION: Croatia

DATES: March 1995 to January 1996

COUNTRIES PARTICIPATING: (38) Argentina, Bangladesh, Belgium, Brazil, Canada, Czech Republic, Denmark, Egypt, Estonia, Finland, France, Germany, Ghana, Indonesia, Ireland, Jordan, Kenya, Lithuania, Malaysia, Nepal, Netherlands, New Zealand, Nigeria, Norway, Pakistan, Poland, Portugal, Russian Federation, Senegal, Slovakia, Spain, Sweden, Switzerland, Tunisia, Turkey, Ukraine, United Kingdom, United States

MAXIMUM STRENGTH: 15,522 (includes 14,663 troops, 328 military observers and 531 civilian police) (1995)

STRENGTH AT WITHDRAWAL: 3,376

FATALITIES: 16   CLASP(S): None

UNPREDEP - United Nations Preventive Deployment Force

COUNTRY/LOCATION: Former Yugoslav Republic of Macedonia

DATES: March 1995 to present

COUNTRIES PARTICIPATING: (32) Argentina, Bangladesh, Belgium, Brazil, Canada, Czech Republic, Denmark, Egypt, Finland, France, Ghana, Indonesia, Ireland, Jordan, Kenya, Malaysia, Nepal, Netherlands, New Zealand, Nigeria, Norway, Pakistan, Poland, Portugal, Russian Federation, Senegal, Spain, Sweden, Switzerland, Ukraine, United Kingdom, United States

MAXIMUM STRENGTH: 1,314 authorized (1,050 troops, 35 military observers and 26 civilian police plus provisions for 76 international staff and 127 locally-recruited civilian staff)

CURRENT STRENGTH: 1,118 troops, 35 military observers and 27 civilian police (1996)

FATALITIES: None (1996)   CLASP(S): None

UNMIBH - United Nations Mission in Bosnia and Herzegovina

COUNTRY/LOCATION: Bosnia and Herzegovina

DATES: December 1995 to present

COUNTRIES PARTICIPATING: (35) Argentina, Austria, Bangladesh, Bulgaria, Denmark, Egypt, Estonia, Fiji, Finland, France, Germany, Ghana, Greece, Hungary, India, Indonesia, Ireland, Jordan, Kenya, Malaysia, Nepal, Netherlands, Norway, Pakistan, Poland, Portugal, Russian Federation, Senegal, Spain, Sweden, Switzerland, Tunisia, Turkey, Ukraine, United States

MAXIMUM STRENGTH: 3,006 authorized (1,721 police monitors, 5 military liaison officers, 380 international staff and 900 locally-recruited staff)

CURRENT STRENGTH: 1,197 police monitors supported by approximately 350 international and locally-recruited staff (1996)

FATALITIES: None (1996) CLASP(S): None

U.S. Air Force Parachutist Insignia

Colonel Donald R. Strobaugh, a leading Air Force parachutist for many years, and a collector of military insignia is in a very small group of veterans who have been able to provide information about the parachutist insignia used by the U.S. Air Force. His excellent account of the Air Force parachute insignia history is provided here as a reference for all of us who have searched for this hard-to-find information.

The current style parachutist badges for USAF qualified personnel are the same as those used by the Army. The current parachutist badge is the same as that used by the Army during World War II. When the Air Force became a separate service in 1947, it continued to use the Army parachute badge. The parachutist badge at that time was mostly worn by USAF Combat Control Team members, test parachutists assigned to El Centro, California and Wright-Patterson Air Force Base, Ohio, and a small number of jumpers assigned to USAF Air Intelligence. In 1955, the Air Force decided that it should have its own distinctive parachute insignia; so, all Air Force parachutist organizations were asked to submit proposals for a new parachute insignia. The proposals that were submitted all had the parachute design within the standard wing insignia worn by Air Force aircrewmen. Three levels of Basic, Senior, and Master were also proposed.

Chief Warrant Officer Larry Lambert, one of the test parachutists at El Centro, California, who had made over 600 jumps and was considered the "Number 1" jumper in the Air Force is credited with contributing to the design of the distinctive USAF parachutist badge. An interesting fact about CWO Lambert is that he made the first test ejection seat jump from a jet in 1946. The final design was in the style of the Medical badges of today. The new badge was adopted by the Air Force in 1956, and the first Master Parachutist Badge was pinned on CWO Lambert by the Secretary of the Air Force in a Pentagon ceremony.

The first badges produced in 1956 were thick, slightly concave, and usually sterling silver; they had nine suspension lines under the canopy. When the supply of these badges was depleted in 1957, a new sterling silver badge was designed as a thinner, flatter badge with only seven suspension lines beneath the canopy. The badges were never authorized to be made in cloth for wear on the fatigue uniform nor were they ever authorized in bullion for wear on the mess dress uniform.

In 1963 the Air Force discontinued its unique and now hard-to-find parachute insignia after listening to many complaints about the badge and never silencing the desire of many for the aviation wing style badge. The Air Force then went back to the previous Army parachutist badge and has continued to wear it since. An original "USAF" distinctive parachutist badge is now a hot item for military memorabilia collectors. Little has been written about this badge which perhaps makes it even more interesting.

Women Airforce Service Pilots (WASP)

As the prospect of war drew closer in 1941, General Henry H. (Hap) Arnold looked for a solution to ease the shortage of male military pilots. The answer to the shortage was in a proposal by famed female aviatrix Jacqueline Cochran to recruit and train women as military pilots. While her initial proposal was rejected, she was later appointed Director of Women's Flying Training Detachment (WFTD) in 1942 by Arnold after the success of the Women's Auxiliary Ferrying Squadron (WAFS). The WAFS was created in September 1942 at New Castle Army Air Base in Wilmington, Delaware to perform ferry duty for the Air Transport Command.

After General Arnold directed the training of women pilots for non-combat flying jobs, recruitment for qualified candidates was begun in earnest. To qualify as a candidate, applicants had to be personally approved by Ms. Cochran after meeting the minimum requirements which were: 1. between the ages of 21 and 25; 2. a high school graduate; 3. a commercial pilot license; 4. at least 200 hours of flight time; and 5. cross country flight experience. Eventually, the requirement for flight time would be reduced to 35 hours because of the availability of qualified candidates.

While the first class of these women pilots graduated on April 28, 1943 in Houston, Texas, it would not be until August of that same year that the WAFS and the WFTD would merge to become the Women Airforce Service Pilots (WASPS). The training would eventually be moved to Avenger Field in Sweetwater, Texas.

The training of women pilots lasted 23 weeks, encompassing 115 hours of flying instruction and 180 hours of ground school. The length of training would later be extended to 30 weeks with 210 hours of flying time and 393 hours of ground school. There were 1,074 graduates of the WASP training program. They would fly numerous aircraft, including the B-17, B-26, B-29, C-47, and C-54.

They were assigned to numerous bases throughout the United States while serving in the Air Transport Command, the Third Air Force, Material Command, the Weather Wing, and the Flying Training Command. Their duties would include ferrying aircraft, towing targets, personnel transport, and experimental flight testing as well as bombardier pilot and navigational training.

On October 3, 1944, the WASP program was ordered to be deactivated on December 20, 1944. The last WASP training class graduated on December 7, 1944. When the Air Force announced that it would train its "first women pilots" in the mid-1970s, the WASP veterans were insulted as they rightfully believe that they had been the first women military pilots! The WAFS and WASP had been hired under Civil Service to speed up the desperately needed training program to provide the pilots necessary for the war effort. As the bill to militarize the WASP went before Congress in 1944, the decision to deactivate the WASP was made and no subsequent action was taken to grant them veteran status until 1977 when Congress recognized the WASP as veterans of the United States Air Force and awarded them the veterans' benefits that they were long overdue. The WASP were an integral and important part of the Air Force' success during World War II.

As graduation approached in 1943 for the first WASP students of the 319th Army Air Force Flight Training Detachment (AAFFTD) in Houston, Texas, detachment officials realized that there were no wings available for presentation to the graduates. So, some distinctive wings were quickly designed by Mrs. Leoti Deaton and Lieutenant Alfred Fleishman --they were crafted out of Army Air Force pilot wings and had a smooth shield instead of the federal shield in the center of the wing. The detachment designation, "319th," was engraved on a scroll that sits atop the shield; later classes would be engraved with "318th" for the 318th AAFFTD. The first WASP class, 43-W-1, had a "W-1" engraved on the shield. Wings for classes, 43-4, 43-5, and 43-6 were made from observer wings when pilot wings were no longer available. The first lozenge style wings were presented to class 43-W-8; they were made with a shiny finish and would be changed to a satin finish for class 44-1. The official WASP wing was similar to the AAF pilot badge except a diamond shaped lozenge replaced the federal shield. The diamond lozenge is a heraldic device that symbolizes unmarried women and widows. The final WASP wing design is said to have been created by Ms Jacqueline Cochran, the key figure in the creation of the WASP.

Miscellaneous Badges

Air Force personnel have been authorized during certain periods to wear certain badges awarded by other military services that they may have received while a member of that service or as a result of completing certain specialized training from that service. Other service regulations should be consulted for exact requirements and authorizations for their specific badges. Foreign badges may also be worn on the uniform as prescribed by current USAF uniform regulations. The Junior AFROTC Instructor Badge is the only one shown here that is applicable solely to the uniform of an USAF retiree. Some of those badges that have been authorized for wear on the Air Force uniform are described here. To ascertain requirements and time periods, readers should consult Air Force regulations for the specific period of interest.

Parachute Rigger

Awarded to individuals who successfully complete the Parachute Rigger course conducted by the U.S. Army Quartermaster School.

Junior AFROTC Instructor Badge

Worn by instructors in the Junior Air Force Reserve Officer Training Corps (AFROTC) program conducted in selected high schools. These programs are conducted by at least one field grade officer (major, lieutenant colonel, colonel) and at least one senior non-commissioned officer (master sergeant, senior master sergeant, chief master sergeant). Large detachments may have additional personnel assigned. Instructors for the JRAFROTC program are retired USAF personnel who are nominated to selected high schools by AFROTC Headquarters and are selected by those schools to manage their JRAFROTC program. These instructors, officially retired from the USAF, continue to wear the USAF uniform with the addition of the JRAFROTC Instructor Badge on the right pocket of the service uniform.

Scuba Badge

Awarded to individuals who have successfully completed appropriate level diver training.

Army General Staff Identification Badge

The Army General Staff ID Badge may be worn as a permanent part of the uniform when the individual has completed at least one year's service on the Army General Staff and has been certified by the Director of the Army Staff as having demonstrated outstanding performance of duty while assigned to the General Staff. Original issue of the badge is made by the Office, Chief of Staff, Army.

Air Assault Badge

Awarded to qualified graduates of the Army's Air Assault School.

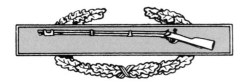

Combat Infantryman Badge (CIB)

The Combat Infantryman Badge was established by the War Department on October 27, 1943. It remains today as one of the most revered badges in the U.S. military. To be awarded the CIB, a soldier must be an infantryman satisfactorily performing infantry duties, must be assigned to an infantry unit when the unit is engaged in ground combat, and must actively participate in the ground combat. Personnel assigned special forces specialty codes are also authorized the CIB under the same conditions. Separate awards of the CIB have been authorized for World War II, the Korean War, and the Vietnam War. Only one award is authorized for service in Vietnam, Laos, the Dominican Republic, Korea (after July 27,1954), Grenada, Panama, and the Persian Gulf War regardless of whether an individual has served one or more tours in one or more of these areas. Second and third awards of the CIB are indicated by superimposing 1 and 2 stars, respectively, centered at the top of the badge between the points of the oak wreath.

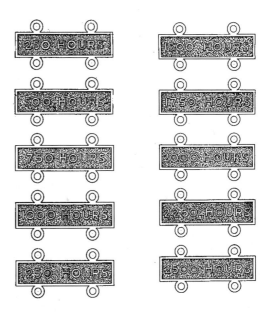

Ground Observers Corps Badge (Rating)

Awarded for so many hours acting as a member of the USAF Ground Observers Corps. This badge was established in 1952.

USAF Honor Guard Hat Badge

Combat Medic Badge (CMB)

Awarded to members (O-6 and below) of the Army Medical Department, the Navy Medical Department, or the Air Force Medical Service assigned or attached to the Army and special forces personnel with designated medical specialty codes who satisfactorily performed medical duties after December 6, 1941 while attached to a medical unit organic to an infantry unit that was engaged in active ground combat. The badge may be awarded for each war as specified in the preceding paragraph for the CIB.

USAF ORDER OF PRECEDENCE OF

1. Medal of Honor	2. Air Force Cross	3. Distinguished Service Cross
4. Navy Cross	5. Defense Distinguished Service Medal	6. Distinguished Service Medal (see note 1)
7. Silver Star	8. Defense Superior Service Medal	9. Legion of Merit
10. Distinguished Flying Cross	11. Airman's Medal	12. Soldier's Medal
13. Navy-Marine Corps Medal	14. Coast Guard Medal	15. Bronze Star Medal
16. Purple Heart	17. Defense Meritorious Service Medal	18. Meritorious Service Medal
19. Air Medal	20. Aerial Achievement Medal	21. Joint Service Commendation Medal
22. Air Force Commendation Medal	23. Army Commendation Medal	24. Navy Commendation Medal
25. Coast Guard Commendation Medal	26. Joint Service Achievement Medal	27. Air Force Achievement Medal
28. Army Achievement Medal	29. Navy Achievement Medal	30. Combat Action Ribbon (see note 2)
31. Distinguished/Presidential Unit Citation	32. Navy Presidential Unit Citation	33. Joint Meritorious Unit Citation
34. AF Outstanding Unit Award	35. AF Organizational Excellence Award	36. Prisoner of War Medal
37. Valorous Unit Award	38. Navy Unit Commendation	39. Coast Guard Unit Commendation
40. Meritorious Unit Commendation (Army/Navy/Coast Guard) (worn in the order earned)	41. Navy "E" Ribbon	42. U.S. Nonmilitary Decorations (see note 3)
43. Combat Readiness Medal	44. AF Good Conduct Medal	45. Army Good Conduct Medal
46. Navy Good Conduct Medal	47. Marine Corps Good Conduct Medal	48. Coast Guard Good Conduct Medal
49. Air Reserve Forces Meritorious Service Medal	50. Army Reserve Component Achievement Medal	51. Naval Reserve Meritorious Service Medal
52. Selected Marine Corps Reserve Medal	53. Coast Guard Reserve Good Conduct Medal	54. Outstanding Airman of the Year Ribbon
55. Air Force Recognition Ribbon	56. China Service Medal	57. American Defense Service Medal
58. Women's Army Corps Service Medal	59. WWII Theater Campaign Medals (see note 4)	60. WWII Victory Medal
61. Occupation Medal (Navy/Army) (worn in the order earned)	62. Medal For Humane Action	63. National Defense Service Medal
64. Korean Service Medal	65. Antarctica Service Medal	66. Armed Forces Expeditionary Medal
67. Vietnam Service Medal	68. Southwest Asia Service Medal	69. Armed Forces Service Medal
70. Humanitarian Service Medal	71. Outstanding Volunteer Service Medal	72. AF Overseas Ribbon (S/L)
73. Army Overseas Ribbon	74. Sea Service Deployment Ribbon (Navy/Marine)	75. Coast Guard Special Operations Service

MULTI-SERVICE DECORATIONS AND AWARDS

76. Coast Guard Sea Service	77. AF Longevity Service Award Ribbon	78. Reserve Medals (Armed Forces/Navy/Marine Corps) (worn in order earned)
79. NCO Professional Military Education Graduate Ribbon	80. Army NCO Professional Development Ribbon	81. USAF BMT Honor Graduate Ribbon
82. Coast Guard Reserve Honor Graduate Ribbon	83. Small Arms Expert Marksmanship Ribbon	84. Navy & Coast Guard Shooting Medals (see note 9)
85. Air Force Training Ribbon	86. Army Service Ribbon	87. Philippine Defense Medal
88. Philippine Liberation Medal	89. Philippine Independence Medal	90. Merchant Marine Combat Bar
91. Merchant Marine War Zone (worn in order earned)	92. Foreign Decorations (see note 6)	93. Philippine Presidential Unit Citation
94. Republic of Korea Presidential Unit Citation	95. Other Foreign Unit Citations (see note 6)	96. United Nations Service Medal (Korea)
97. United Nations Medal	98. NATO Medal	99. Multilateral Organization Awards (see note 8)
100. Inter-American Defense Board Medal	101. Republic of Vietnam Campaign Medal	102. Kuwait Liberation Medal (Saudi Arabia)
103. Kuwait Liberation Medal (Kuwait)	104. Foreign Service Medals (see note 7)	

NOTES:

1. Wear the AF Distinguished Service Medal (DSM) ahead of a Distinguished Service Medal awarded by the Army, Navy, and Coast Guard.

2. Awarded only by the Navy, Marine Corps and Coast Guard.

3. A few of the decorations awarded by federal agencies are: Medal of Merit, National Security Medal, Presidential Medal of Freedom, Medal of Freedom, Gold and Silver Lifesaving Medals, NASA Distinguished Service Medal, Public Health Service Decorations (Distinguished Service Medal, Meritorious Service Medal, Commendation Medal); US Maritime Service Decorations (Distinguished Service Medal, Meritorious Service Medal, Mariner's Medal). Do not wear these decorations unless you wear US military decorations and service medals. If you wear more than one, arrange them in the order of acceptance. If you wear two or more from the same agency, that agency decides the precedence. Ribbons must be the same size as AF ribbons. Wear only those decoration ribbons awarded by federal agencies and earned while in military service.

4. The American Campaign Medal, Asiatic-Pacific Campaign Medal, and European-African-Middle Eastern Campaign Medal are WWII Theater Campaign Medals. If authorized more than one, wear them in the order earned.

5. When awarded more than one clasp, wear in the order earned on the suspension ribbon. Do not wear clasps on the service ribbon.

6. Do not wear these decorations unless you wear other US military decorations and service medals. When authorized more than one, wear in the order earned. If authorized more than one from the same foreign country, wear them in the order the country prescribes. On special occasions and as a matter of courtesy to a given country, you may wear the decorations of that country ahead of all other foreign decorations.

7. Before you wear foreign service ribbons, meet conditions in AFI 36-2803 (formerly AFR 900-48). When authorized to wear more than one, wear them in the order earned.

8. Includes ribbons such as: Multinational Force Observers Medal and Inter-American Defense Board Medal. Wear these ribbons in the order earned and ensure they are the same size as Air Force Ribbons.

9. Precedence is Navy Expert Rifle Medal, Navy Expert Pistol Medal, Coast Guard Expert Rifle Medal, Coast Guard Expert Pistol Medal.

THE UNITED STATES OF AMERICA

TO ALL WHO SHALL SEE THESE PRESENTS, GREETING:

THIS IS TO CERTIFY THAT
THE PRESIDENT OF THE UNITED STATES OF AMERICA
AUTHORIZED BY ACT OF CONGRESS JULY 2, 1926
HAS AWARDED

THE DISTINGUISHED FLYING CROSS

TO

CAPTAIN

FOR
EXTRAORDINARY ACHIEVEMENT
WHILE PARTICIPATING IN AERIAL FLIGHT

31 OCTOBER 1972

GIVEN UNDER MY HAND IN THE CITY OF WASHINGTON
THIS 25TH DAY OF APRIL 19 74

Leroy J. Manor
MAJOR GENERAL, USAF

John L. McLucas
SECRETARY OF THE AIR FORCE

AF FORM 2249, JUL 70

THE UNITED STATES OF AMERICA

TO ALL WHO SHALL SEE THESE PRESENTS, GREETING:

THIS IS TO CERTIFY THAT
THE PRESIDENT OF THE UNITED STATES OF AME
AUTHORIZED BY EXECUTIVE ORDER, MAY 11, 194
HAS AWARDED

THE AIR MEDAL
(THIRD OAK LEAF CLUSTER)

TO

CAPTAIN

FOR
MERITORIOUS ACHIEVEMENT
WHILE PARTICIPATING IN AERIAL FLIGHT

10 AUGUST 1972 TO 9 OCTOBER 1972

GIVEN UNDER MY HAND IN THE CITY OF WASHINGTON
THIS 28TH DAY OF NOVEMBER 19 72

G. Johnson
G. W. JOHNSON, Lt General, USAF
Commander, 8th Air Force

Robt C. Se
SECRETARY OF THE AIR

AF FORM 2232, JUL 70

DEPARTMENT OF THE AIR FORCE

THIS IS TO CERTIFY THAT

THE AIR FORCE ACHIEVEMENT MEDAL

HAS BEEN AWARDED TO

LIEUTENANT

FOR

OUTSTANDING ACHIEVEMENT

20 MAY 1991 TO 30 MAY 1992

ACCOMPLISHMENTS

Lieutenant   distinguished himself by outstanding
achievement as Chairman, 75th Anniversary Grand March, Chanute Air Force Base,
Illinois.   meticulously planned and executed all details of the
march involving over 2,500 personnel, both military and civilian. Distinguished military and civilian guests, as well as the local civilian and mili-
ary populace, praised the event as one of the largest, most stirring, and
patriotic events in Chanute's history. The personal dedication of
   to make the Grand March a resounding success and a worthy tribute to
Chanute's 75 years of contributions to the military and civilian communities
reflects credit upon himself and the United States Air Force.

GIVEN UNDER MY HAND THIS   13TH   DAY OF   JULY   19 92

RKMcLeod
ROBERT K. McLEOD, Colonel, USAF
Vice Commander, Chanute Training Center
Chanute Air Force Base, Illinois

AF FORM 2274, FEB 92
PREVIOUS EDITION WILL BE USED

Foreign Award Certificates

NATO Medal Award Certificate

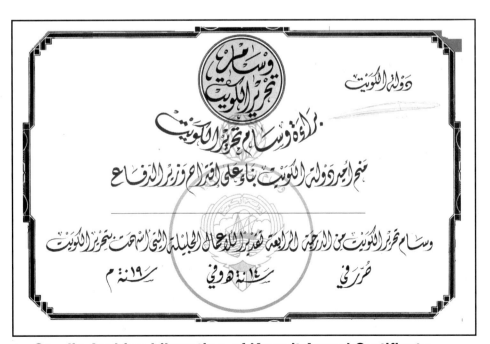

Saudia Arabian Liberation of Kuwait Award Certificate

USAF Ribbon Mount Formats

Service ribbbons are worn in order of precedence from the wearer's right to their left or as the Navy says "from inbound to outbound".The ribbons are normally worn in rows of 3 with no space between multiple rows.

If the service coat lapel covers any of the ribbons on upper rows the ribbons may be worn in a row of 4. Examples of the various combinations are shown below.

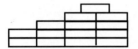 

If the service coat lapel covers any of the ribbons on upper rows the ribbons may be worn in a row of 4.

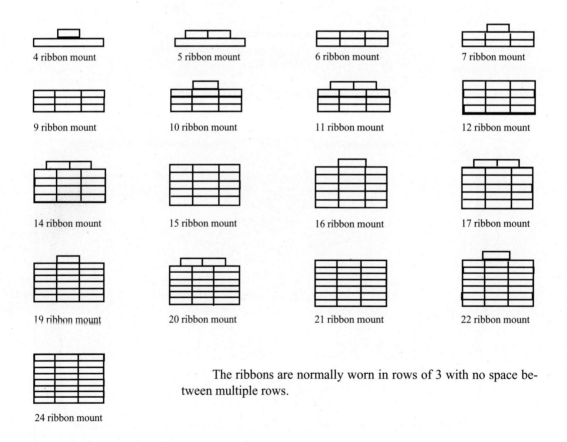

4 ribbon mount	5 ribbon mount	6 ribbon mount	7 ribbon mount
9 ribbon mount	10 ribbon mount	11 ribbon mount	12 ribbon mount
14 ribbon mount	15 ribbon mount	16 ribbon mount	17 ribbon mount
19 ribbon mount	20 ribbon mount	21 ribbon mount	22 ribbon mount
24 ribbon mount			

The ribbons are normally worn in rows of 3 with no space between multiple rows.

Bibliography

Borts, Lawrence. *United Nations Medals and Missions*, 1997.

Campbell, J. Duncan. *Aviation Badges and Insignia of the United States Army*, 1913-1946, 1977.

Dept. of Defense Manual DOD 1348.33M. *Manual of Military Decorations and Awards*, 1993.

Foster, Frank and Borts, Lawrence. *U.S. Military Medals 1939 To Present, 3rd ed.*, 1995.

Foster, Frank and Sylvester, John. *The Decorations and Medals of the Republic of Vietnam and Her Allies, 1950-1975,* 1995.

Kerrigan, E. *American Medals and Decorations*, 1990.

Maguire, Jon A. *Silver Wings, Pinks and Greens*, 1994.

Morgan, J.L. Pete and Thurman, Ted A. *American Military Patch Guide*, 1997.

Official Guide to the Army Air Forces. Simon and Schuster, 1944.

Ogletree, Maj Larry. *"The Missile Badge,"* 1996.

Oliver, Ray. *"What's In A Name?,"* 1983.

Rosignoli, Guido. *Badges and Insignia of World War II*, 1980.

Smith, Richard W. *Shoulder Sleeve Insignia of the U.S. Armed Forces*, 1981.

Spink, Barry L. *"A Chronology of the Enlisted Rank Chevron of the United Statess Air Force,"* 1992.

Strandberg, J.E. and Bender, R.J. *The Call to Duty*, 1994.

Strobaugh, Donald R. *"U.S. Air Force Parachutist Insignia, 1956 - 1963."* 1980.

U.S. Air Force Instruction 11-402 - Aviation Service, Aeronautical Ratings and Badges, 1994.

U.S. Air Force Instruction 36-2803 - The Air Force Awards and Decorations Program, 1994.

U.S. Air Force Instruction 36-2903 - Dress and Personal Appearance of Air Force Personnel, 1994.

U.S. Air Force Instruction 36-2923 - Aeronautical, Duty, and Occupational Badges, 1994.

U.S. Air Force Regulation 35-5 - Missile Badges, 1966.

U.S. Air Force Regulation 50-43 - USAF Small Arms Marksmanship Badge, 1992.

U.S. Air Force Regulation 125-3. Security Police, 1975.

U.S. Air Force Regulation 900-21 - Air Weapons Controller Badge, 1985.

U.S. Air Force Regulation 900-39 - Explosive Ordnance Disposal Badge, 1978.

U.S. Air Force Regulation 900-48 - Awards, Ceremonies and Honors, 1982 & 1989.

U.S. Army Regulation 600-35, 1944.

U.S. Army Regulation 672-5 - Military Awards, 1990.

Warnick, A. Timothy. *USAF Combat Medals, Streamers, and Campaigns*, 1990.

Index

Medals of America Press
Proudly presents

The Decorations, Medals, Badges and Insignia of the U.S. Air Force "The First 50 Years" 1947-1997

Lt. Col. Tony Aldebol, a DFC winner, provides the most comprehensive and lavishly illustrated work on all of the Decorations, Medals, Badges and Insignia of the AAF and USAF. If you can have only one book on the Air Force, this is it. Loaded with illustrations and details, this is the most complete work ever done. Complete color plates of all medals, ribbons, badges, insignia and ranks.
120 pages. 8 1/2 x 11 inches with 16 color plates.
Hardback ISBN: 1-884452-20-5   Retail price $24.95
Softback ISBN: 1-884452-21-3   Retail price $19.95

United Nations Medals and Missions

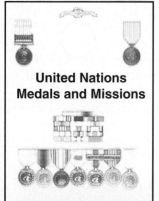

The Dean of American Ribbons, Lonny Borts, has produced another masterpiece in the first complete book on all United Nations medals, ribbons and the missions that generated them. Complete color plates of all medals and ribbons with tables depicting which country served in each mission. Explanation of the meaning of each medal ribbon and complete description of each mission and participants. Special section on all the UN Korean medals. The only work of it's type in the world today.
96 pages. 8 1/2 x 11 inches with 16 color plates.
Hardback ISBN: 1-884452-31-0   Retail price $24.95
Softback ISBN: 1-884452-30-2   Retail price $19.95

Decorations, Medals, Ribbons, Badges and Insignia of the United States Marine Corps - World War II to Present

Captain James Thompson presents the most thorough and easy to use guide on the Decorations, Medals, Ribbons, Badges and Insignia of the U.S. Marine Corps. Complete with beautifully illustrated color plates, this book will prove to be your single source for information dating from World War II to the present. First book of its type ever published in the USA.
112 pages. 8 1/2 x 11 inches with 16 color plates.
Hardback ISBN: 1-884452-39-6   Retail price $24.95
Softback ISBN: 1-884452-38-8   Retail price $19.95

American Military Patch Guide

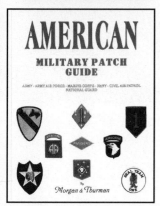

The single most complete source on United States military patches presented by Major Pete Morgan and Ted Thurman. Special sections lay out complete color displays of Army, Navy, Marine, Air Force, and Army Air Force patches with identifying text.The color plates illustrate and identify approximately 2,000 patches and tabs in full color. Covers WW 2 to present.
96 pages. 8 1/2 x 11 inches.
Hardback ISBN: 1-884452-33-7   Retail price $29.95
Softback ISBN: 1-884452-32-9   Retail price $24.95

Coming soon "Medals of Indochina"

Write or call Medals of America Press 1929 Fairview Road, Fountain Inn, SC 29644
E mail Medals@USMedals.com   web site HTTP://WWW.USMEDALS.COM
Telephone: (864) 862-6051 Fax: (864) 862-0256

Medals of America Press

Proudly presents

U.S. Military Medals 1939 to Present (New 3rd Edition)

America's best selling book on military medals. The most complete, easy to use guide to the last 50 years of United States Decorations and Service Medals. Full-color plates with text show all U.S. medals, ribbons and commonly awarded foreign medals. Special sections lay out complete color displays of Army, Navy, Marine, Air Force, Coast Guard and Merchant Marine awards with identifying text. Additional sections cover the history, wear, display, procurement and devices worn on U.S. awards.

3rd Edition. 80 pages. 8 1/2 x 11 inches with 16 color plates.
Hardback ISBN: 1-884452-12-4   Retail price $24.95
Softback ISBN: 1-884452-13-2   Retail price $19.95

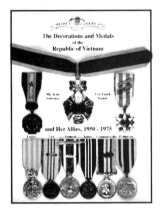

The Decorations and Medals of the Republic of Vietnam and Her Allies 1950 - 1975

This is the finest and most complete guide to all Republic of Vietnam military and civilian decorations, medals, ribbons and unit awards. It covers RVN awards from the beginning of the State to the fall of the Republic. Over 110 Vietnamese medals are displayed in full color. Awards are listed by both English and Vietnamese names. Also includes full color plates and descriptions of all the period medals of the South Vietnamese Allies.

96 pages. 8 1/2 x 11 inches, hardback with 16 color plates.
Hardback ISBN: 1-884452-02-7   Retail price $24.95

The Military Ribbons of the United States Army, Navy, Marines, Air Force, and Coast Guard - A Complete Guide to Correct Ribbon Wear

This color booklet has the complete order of precedence for every ribbon of the Armed Forces presented by individual branch of service. Each ribbon is identified in full color and displayed in correct order for each service. Facing pages depict what ribbon devices go on each ribbon. This book is the perfect reference for veterans and active duty as well as collectors. The last 60 years (1939 to 1997) are covered in this guide.

12 pages. 8 1/2 x 11 inches.
Retail price $5.00

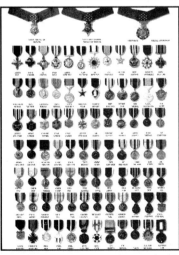

United States Medals Chart

This full color chart is the most up to date chart available for United States Military Medals from World War II to the present. Each medal is shown in beautiful detail in full size along with a brief description under each medal name. Additionally, the most commonly awarded foreign medals to American veterans are also displayed. The chart has been reviewed by the Institute of Heraldry for correct order of precedence. Printed on 100 pound gloss enamel and varnished for added protection. It frames beautifully at 25 x 38 inches.

Write or call Medals of America Press 1929 Fairview Road, Fountain Inn, SC 29644
E mail Medals@USMedals.com   web site HTTP://WWW.USMEDALS.COM
Telephone: (864) 862-6051   Fax: (864) 862-0256

Notes